Quilted Memories

If I were a Star
I would be a ballerina
I would be happy
and I would smile
I would smile For
my mom.

For the —
I love being
your friend,
you rock &
make me
smile !
Lesley Riley

Quilted Memories

JOURNALING, SCRAPBOOKING & CREATING
KEEPSAKES WITH FABRIC

Lesley Riley

Sterling Publishing Co., Inc. New York
A Sterling/Chapelle Book

Book Design: Rose Sheifer

Photographer: Ryne Hazen

Chapelle, Ltd.: P.O. Box 9252, Ogden, UT 84409

(801) 621-2777 • (801) 621-2788 Fax
e-mail: chapelle@chapelleltd.com
Web site: www.chapelleltd.com

Library of Congress Cataloging-in-Publication Data

Riley, Lesley.
  Quilted memories : journaling, scrapbooking & creating keepsakes with fabric / Lesley Riley.
       p. cm.
  "A Sterling/Chapelle Book."
  Includes index.
  ISBN 1-4027-1484-X
1. Patchwork. 2. Quilting. 3. Assemblage (Art) I. Title.

TT835.R539 2005
745.58'2--dc22
                                                          2004025732

10 9 8 7 6 5 4 3 2 1

Published by Sterling Publishing Co., Inc.
387 Park Avenue South, New York, NY 10016
©2005 by Lesley Riley
Distributed in Canada by Sterling Publishing
c/o Canadian Manda Group, 165 Dufferin Street
Toronto, Ontario, Canada M6K 3H6
Distributed in Great Britain by Chrysalis Books Group PLC,
The Chrysalis Building, Bramley Road, London W10 6SP, England
Distributed in Australia by Capricorn Link (Australia) Pty. Ltd.
P. O. Box 704, Windsor, NSW 2756, Australia
Printed and Bound in China
All Rights Reserved

Sterling ISBN 1-4027-1484-X

Contents

Dedication

To my parents, for raising me to believe I could do anything I set my mind to. They gave me wings. To my husband Buddy and our children, Brian, Sara, Chris, Sam, Kerry, and Kelly. They never cease to give me the love, support, and opportunity to spread my wings.

Acknowledgments

First, I would like to thank the artists who so generously took time from their busy schedules to share their ideas and inspiration in the quilts they made for this book. Their contributions are invaluable to us all. Thanks to Cindy Stoeckl at Chapelle, Ltd., for being my first link to the world of publishing, and to Jo Packham and all of the decision makers at Chapelle, Ltd. and Sterling Publishing Company Inc., who believed in me as a first-time author.

A special thanks to Matthew DeMaio and Lecia Monsen for helping me turn my vision into a reality.

Introduction

Making art is an unending source of surprise, delight and pleasure. It is the alchemy of turning everyday materials into gold, the act of making something of beauty out of these everyday materials that never ceases to amaze me. I want to share this magic with you.

Whether you consider yourself a quilter or collage artist, a scrapbooker or the creator of mixed media and assemblage, this book is intended for you. It is for you because the bottom line is that we all enjoy the process of making art and we really don't need to define ourselves by any word other than artist. It is by the exposure to other arts and the sharing of methods and materials that we all grow and improve as artists. When we learn and borrow from other art arenas it makes our art richer. Art history is ripe with borrowing and imitation; but ultimately we have to mirror our own soul in what we create, because the purpose of creating, the reason we do it is the drive for self-expression. Unless we fulfill that need, we ourselves will not be fulfilled.

I'm a consummate reader but I'm always at a loss for words when I attempt to express what I feel through writing. Yet I never have a problem finding photos and fabrics that speak for me, helping me to express some of my deepest thoughts, memories, and feelings. I believe that photographs, colors, and even certain patterns and textures of fabric can lead to memories or

ideas that many of us share in common—memories and concepts that are hard to put into words, like home, comfort, innocence; or courage, wisdom, and joy.

I'm delighted to share with you how I work and what I have learned in my journey as an artist and quilter. Because many teachers are better than one, I'll also introduce you to other artists who work with image and text. Together we hope to share with you a bit of the magic we call art.

HOW TO USE THIS BOOK

The techniques and ideas in this book are intended to assist you in re-creating your own memories and ideas in fabric. In describing how to make the quilts, I've tried to explain the thought processes of each artist and why certain design decisions were made—decisions that reinforce the original intent and inspiration for the quilt. It is not my intention that you try to re-create each quilt as shown. Rather, I've provided the materials and methods to help you construct your own versions, using your own photographs, fabrics, and memories along with the inspiration and techniques I hope you will find within these pages.

Throughout these pages I will introduce you to new methods and materials for producing quilts. As a reformed perfectionist, I learned a long time ago (with the aid of my six children), that life is more rewarding if you accept and embrace the imperfections that come your way. In doing so, I discovered that imperfections add character. It is the act of playing with fabric without worrying about rules and perfect stitches that has allowed me to create with an abandon that is evident in the art I make.

Yet there is still a need for attention to certain details. My design school training taught me that poor craftsmanship will detract from even the best designed and most heartfelt piece. Because I want my work to look well crafted, I have created

I have always been delighted at the prospect of a new day, a fresh try, one more start, with perhaps a bit of magic waiting somewhere behind the morning.

JB Priestley

new techniques to simplify processes that I find difficult or time-consuming, especially new methods for finishing your quilt.

For many quilters, this book is intended to get you to think outside the box. How do you get outside the box? I hope this book will be your ticket out. The quilts and the time involved to make them are small. The emphasis is on exploring and re-creating an idea, a memory, or a moment. This is your chance to play.

For nonquilters, hopefully I will inspire you to think about quilts as another opportunity to explore mixed media. Above all, I want everyone to have fun and play your way to making some wonderful quilted collage art. The best advice I can give you is to stop thinking and just start.

This book is your permission to break the rules, whether they are self-imposed or have been carried with you since grade school art classes. It is my intention to show you many ways to use materials and techniques that will, in turn, spark your own ideas and inspiration. If I have done my job well, you will not stop with what you discover between the covers of this book, but will be inspired to try other things or further investigate processes that are mentioned but not covered in depth. I have provided a Reference section of authors and magazines on pages 126–127 that includes sources I turn to time and again for inspiration and information.

JUST A DREAM.

Getting Started

LEARNING HOW TO SEE
LIKE AN ARTIST

When I was a young quilter in the 1970s, I came across the concept of learning how to "see like an artist." It sounded so magical and mysterious. Could artists actually see differently than the rest of us? What did they see that they were able to translate into their art? They were obviously seeing something that I wasn't, because my work lacked the magic that I found in so many other artist's work. I wanted to be an artist and find out what they saw. I figured if I could just read enough or look at enough work, that I would discover what it was they were seeing.

Nothing I read, no one I talked to, could tell me how an artist saw, so I kept studying and searching for the answer. I took classes in design, I studied classical oil painting, and I apprenticed with an interior design firm. I made quilts from complex patterns and read everything I could on how other artists worked. I was immersed in art and design, and one day it dawned on me—I was seeing design in everything.

That is why I hope you'll take the time to learn and understand the concepts of design. A good sense of design is like any other skill you study to master. Athletes and musicians know that to become proficient in their passion they must practice the basic skills, the free throws and the scales, the warm-ups and the exercises. If you refer to and conscientiously use the elements and principles of design whenever you make art, over time your sense of composition and design will become an automatic part of your way of thinking and creating. It is then, that you too will see like an artist.

I've attempted to explain design terms to you in a way that I found was the easiest for me to understand. The way I learned to use them was by observation, by taking a work of art that appealed to my own sense of design and dissecting it to see where and how the design principles and elements were applied.

The soul of creativity is looking at one thing and seeing another, making surprising connections between things, generating unusual possibilities.

John Chaffee, PhD

Above all, watch with glittering eyes the whole world around you, because the greatest secrets are always hidden in the most unlikely places. Those who don't believe in magic will never find it.

Roald Dahl

I can't teach you to be an artist; all I can do is help you learn to see.

J. P. Loveless

DESIGN

What's wonderful about design is that it's not something we must dream up; it is the look of the world we live in. . . . There are physical properties (shapes, colors, textures), and hidden intangibles (history, tradition, character).

Unknown

Design is manipulating materials to express ideas. It's the road map, the blueprint, the organization of your work of art. Design is problem solving, making decisions at every step that will reinforce the idea you wish to communicate.

The *elements* of design are the *tools* with which you construct the framework for your quilt. Your choice of design elements integrate your materials with your subject and the emotional content of your quilt—and ultimately define your artistic style.

The *principles* of design are the *rules* that you apply to the elements of design to organize your quilt into a unified whole. You select design principles to reinforce the expressive idea you wish to communicate and rely on the dominance of one element or principle to establish unity.

Design principles are the visual elements that give structure to expression. Technique is a means to get where you're going. Many quilts are extremely well made but are predictable and lack interest. Design principles, successfully applied, will set well-crafted quilts apart. Learning a few of the most important design elements will go a long way toward making your quilt stand out in a crowd. Good art is a combination of well-executed design, content, and technique.

ELEMENTS OF DESIGN	PRINCIPLES OF DESIGN
Line	Repetition
Shape/Form	Variety
Value/Light/Contrast	Balance
Texture	Rhythm
Pattern	Dominance
Space	Proportion/Scale
Time/Movement	Unity
Color	Harmony

Exercise

Find a few works of art that you like and make photocopies. With pencil or marker in hand, and your list of design elements and principles by your side, draw in the path your eye takes when looking at the piece; circle each time you find a shape repeated; mark an X over the focal point. Continue to analyze each work to discover how and where design is employed. Now do you get the picture?

IDYLL AUF DEM LANDE — IDYLLE CHAMPÊTRE   phot. J. Gaberell.

It's hard to discuss the elements and principles of design because they are so interrelated. They are always working together in a piece of artwork. They borrow from each other as well: line can have shape; light can have pattern. To improve your sense of design, you should become familiar with what each element and principle is, recognize them when they are applied, and learn to apply them yourself. Let's look at them one by one.

ELEMENTS OF DESIGN

Line

Line is the path of a point moving through space. Line has:
    Shape: straight, curved, diminishing, crooked
    Texture: woolly, silky, wiry, thorny, nubby
    Pattern: net, braid, stripe, knot, lace, chain
    Movement: spiral, zigzag, stretching, drooping, flowing

Shape/Form

Shape may be defined as a closed two- or three-dimensional figure described or delineated by an edge; a separate visual unit, e.g. heart, circle, square. Shapes are two-dimensional, forms are three-dimensional. Shape/Form has:
    Type: symmetrical, squat, elongated, distorted, angular
    Relationship: overlapping, interlocking, surrounding, clustered, divided
    Surface: velvety, padded, beaded, rough, smooth

Value/Light/Contrast

Value refers to the relative lightness or darkness of areas in a design. A study of value is a study in contrasts. Your fabric should be chosen with regard to value. Value contrasts establish what we see. Your eye goes to white first. Lighter colors read larger, darker colors as smaller or receding. Fabrics of like value will be perceived as one value from a distance. In order to see values better, squint at your fabrics. Do they all blend together, or do you see contrasts in light, dark, and medium tones?

Using all three tones—light, dark, and medium—plus a highlight creates interest, holds the eye, and directs it over the quilt. Value/Light/Contrast has:
    Intensity: smoky, frosted, translucent, dazzling
    Movement: reflections, sparkles, shimmers, twinkles

Strong color and angles of the red line contrasts with the softness of the transferred image

Contrast in texture, shape, pattern, and color in the vertical lines adds interest

Texture

Texture is the tactile and visual surface of an object. In a quilt, this influences the mood, character, or impact of the work. Texture includes not only the actual fabric, but what is applied to it, like buttons, beads, or quilting stitches. Texture enhances the message you are trying to convey.

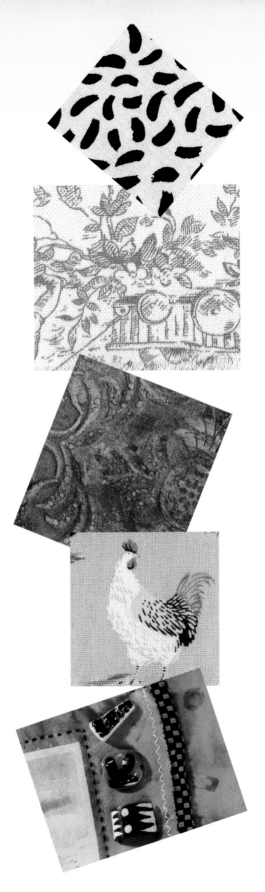

Pattern

Pattern (or lack of it) will be found in the fabrics you choose and in the embellishments you add. You can also create and control pattern by repetition of all of the other elements of design. The importance of pattern is in what it conveys to the quilt's overall design sense. Pattern is not always determined by a printed fabric. Many prints are read from a distance as solids of one color. Step back and squint. Does it have the impact you intended? Pattern can be:

Calm: solids, small-scale prints, straight lines, symmetrical

Busy: large-scale prints, florals, strong contrasting colors, asymmetrical

Space

Space is the boundless expanse within which all things are contained. The area occupied by shapes is called positive space, the areas between shapes is negative space. Space is a design element that occurs through the use of the other elements, but can be controlled by changing placement, altering shapes, or catching light.

Space can also refer to the amount of space your quilt occupies. A large quilt taking up a lot of space creates a different impact than a small one would. Use occupation of space to further your message. Georgia O'Keefe started painting big flowers because she was an unknown; she figured that if she painted small flowers no one would notice, but that they might notice the big ones.

On the other hand, working very small will draw viewers up to your work because they have to get close to see it. Once you've caught their attention, you need to follow through with design that will hold their interest.

Time/Movement

Time and movement are implied in a quilt. Playing with light and color can create the visual effects of movement, as well as actual objects or fabric and threads that may move when someone passes by. Additionally, a quilt can invite the viewer to open or close something to encourage movement.

The passing of time can be conveyed by using certain techniques that suggest age, such as timeworn fabrics, vintage memorabilia, or aging techniques. Careful attention to these details engages viewers and takes them back in time.

COLOR

Color is so important that it deserves its own section. Color theory, based on scientific observations, can be complex. The good news is that you can use color on a personal and intuitive level without understanding all that theory. However, it is helpful to know some basics to assist you in making design decisions. Learn the rules and then feel free to break them: unexpected color combinations can be exciting, and the colors you use can be a mark of personal style.

Color Properties

Color is made up of three distinct visual properties: hue, value, and intensity.

Hue: the specific name for a color, another word for color
Value: the relative lightness or darkness of a color
Intensity: the relative brightness or dullness of a color

The word "relative" in the above definitions is important. All colors work in relation to one another. While a color may appear to be very bright by itself, it can appear dull when it is placed next to another color. Adjacent colors can absorb the light from the color you had planned on being your bright spot.

The color wheel is a helpful guide in using colors. It is based on the grouping of primary colors, secondary colors, and tertiary colors. These colors are arranged on a 12-hue color wheel on page 15.

Other color terminology defines the relationship of these colors to one another and their location on the color wheel. One of my favorite tricks in working with the color wheel is to

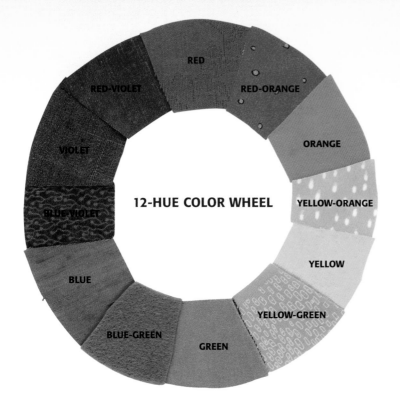

12-HUE COLOR WHEEL

RED
RED-VIOLET
RED-ORANGE
VIOLET
ORANGE
BLUE-VIOLET
YELLOW-ORANGE
BLUE
YELLOW
BLUE-GREEN
YELLOW-GREEN
GREEN

PRIMARY COLORS:
Red, Blue, Yellow.
These colors are primary because they cannot be mixed from any other colors.

SECONDARY COLORS:
Orange (Red + Yellow), Green (Blue + Yellow), Violet (Red + Blue).
Secondary colors result from mixing two primary colors.

TERTIARY COLORS:
Yellow-orange, Red-orange, Red-violet, Blue-violet, Blue-green, Yellow-green.
Tertiary colors are the result of mixing a primary and a secondary color.

find the color opposite the color of the fabric I am using and then choose a fabric in the color next to the one that is opposite. This slight variation in complementary color adds more visual interest.

Color can create mood and tension, e.g. serene blues, fiery reds. It can connote symbolism, e.g. patriotic red, white, and blue, or holiday green and red. Lack of color can put emphasis on another aspect of your quilt, while a riot of color can either excite and entertain or overstimulate and confuse the viewer.

Fabric is your color palette. If you have a stash of fabric, it is usually comprised of your favorite colors and patterns. In order to use color as a design element, you need to have a range of colors, values, and pattern scales. Love blue, hate orange? Orange is the very color that will make your blue sing. Afraid of bright colors? Are all your fabrics of the same value (squint at your stash)? Go buy or create more fabric to round out your stash. While looking for color, don't forget texture. Look for fabrics other than cottons to round out your stash.

Sometimes you may want to create a quilt where the message is color, or a series of quilts working with different aspects of color or different color combinations. Playing with

BASIC COLOR VOCABULARY

Complementary colors
Located across from each other on the wheel

Analogous colors
Located adjacent to each other on the wheel

Triad colors
Three colors located equidistant from each other on the wheel

Warm colors
The range from red to yellow

Cool colors
The range from green to violet

Monochromatic color
One color varying in value and intensity

Tint
A color mixed with white

Shade
A color mixed with black

color and seeing the effects created are instructive lessons. Study other quilters' use of color. What catches your eye? When is color contributing to the work? When does it detract? How could the use of different colors improve the quilt?

PRINCIPLES OF DESIGN

Repetition

The eye loves to follow repetition. Repeating touches of an accent color or shape all over the quilt—whether it be a bead, button, or part of the fabric—makes the eye dance all over the work.

Variety

It's the spice of life, right? It creates viewer interest. Variety is established by contrast in sizes, colors, shapes, textures, and lines—design elements.

Balance

Relating to repetition, colors, shapes, and sizes, balance connotes a sense of even distribution. Balance can be symmetrical or asymmetrical. A symmetrical quilt with obvious balance is sometimes less interesting than one in which equilibrium is maintained among unequal placement. A visually unbalanced quilt in which all of the emphasis is placed on one area, while the rest of the quilt lacks interest, causes unease or disinterest in the viewer.

Rhythm

A feeling of organized movement, rhythm usually involves repetition and balance.

Dominance

This is also known as emphasis: creation of a focal point, a center of interest. In a traditional quilt, the overall repetition of pattern can be the focal point. Dominance can be color, shape, size, or even texture if these are out of ordinary viewer expectations. If a photograph of someone is used in a quilt, it will automatically become the focal point. It is our natural reaction to first look at the human form. Dominance is what is used to catch the viewer's eye, to emphasize your message.

choosing the colors to play off and enhance one another probably requires as much time as the technical aspects. For me colors have a voice, a vibration that sings. When I combine them, they must sing in perfect harmony.

Akira Blount

A Few Things To Keep In Mind When Working With Color

- Don't use colors in equal amounts.

- Squint at your fabric choices before beginning the quilt. Do all the colors blend together? Is there a color spark to delight the viewer's eye? Does the blue-and-red print appear to be red when viewed from a distance, when what you wanted was more blue?

- Don't worry about color schemes. Almost any combination of colors can work well together as long as they are used in the right proportions.

- The greater the number of colors in the fabric or the quilt, the busier it will look. Use color wisely. Often, less says more.

- Sure it's your favorite color, but does it contribute to the overall look of the quilt?

- Yes, you hate that color, but would it add the spark you need to catch your viewer's eye?

Proportion/Scale

The result of comparative relationships. This occurs on three levels: 1) within one part, 2) among parts, 3) between part and whole. Proportion influences whether a shape seems stable and solid, or wispy and sinuous. Usually, the more equal the proportions, the more stable the object seems. The more extreme the proportions, the more interest is engaged.

Scale is the comparative relationship of size regardless of shape. Scale has to do with the correct size and proportion of materials, including weight, texture, pattern, and colors. Choose your fabrics to the scale of your quilt to enhance the reality you are trying to create.

Unity

Unity is achieved when all parts of the quilt work together to achieve a feeling of completeness. Your goal: when the quilt would look no better with the addition of anything else, nor would it look complete with the subtraction of anything. When nothing unintended stands out, when nothing is lost, when you have accomplished what you have set out to do, unity is achieved. Unity is closely tied to composition, the arrangement of artistic parts to form a unified whole.

Harmony

A feeling of agreement. It goes hand in hand with unity. It's a pleasing combination of different elements used in similar ways around a common theme.

10 Most Common Composition Mistakes

1. Unintegrated elements leading the eye off the quilt
2. Too much or too little empty space (too bare or too cluttered)
3. No, or too few, connections (items touching, items relating)
4. Static background (too predictable)
5. Not enough variation of elements (too uninteresting).
6. Unclear focal point/emphasis (what's the point of this quilt?)
7. Not enough contrast of value (all colors perceived as the same from a distance)
8. Lack of balance (feeling of unease)
9. Confused eye movement (where should I look?)
10. Too much technique, not enough content (technique should be secondary to meaning)

THINGS TO DO WITH DESIGN ELEMENTS AND PRINCIPLES

add	fade	layer	reduce	tease
break	fracture	magnify	reverse	undo
combine	grid	multiply	sharpen	variegate
cut	hide	nestle	soften	weave
distort	intersect	overlap	stretch	yellow
divide	join	pattern	substitute	zigzag
exaggerate	knot	quilt	subtract	zoom in

Style

One of the goals in life is to try and be in touch with one's most personal themes— the values, ideas, styles, colors that are the touchstones of one's own individual life, its real texture and substance.
Gloria Vanderbilt

Style is the imprint of your personality on your art. If you allow yourself to work from your heart, your own style will emerge in time. Your work will be as unique as you are. It can't help but be, because nobody has seen the world through your eyes, lived your experiences, or felt your emotions.

Not having your own style is usually a result of two things: 1) not enough courage to create from your true self—your own vision, 2) not enough time spent working on your own ideas. If you work consistently on your own art, your style will come forth effortlessly. In fact, you cannot create a style. It cannot be forced. It is something that *emerges* while you are going about your heart's work.

Style can be imparted with colors, materials, patterns, and signature techniques as well as many other things. Don't try using bits and pieces of someone else's style knowingly. You will always be influenced by other artists' work, but let it register on a subconscious level. Drown yourself in visual images from all types of art, especially before going to bed. Sleep is a fertile time for your subconscious to develop images and ideas.

Here's the good news—you already do have a personal style! It's evidenced by the way you dress, the way you decorate your home. Look at what you surround yourself with. What colors keep appearing? Do you favor solids, florals, cutting-edge design? Do you love embellishment or simplicity? You will be most comfortable developing your own style if you can define what type of design elements and principles you already employ. Take a look in your closet, walk around your house. Make a list of what you see as it relates to design elements and principles.

Another method to assist you in developing your own style is to truly study as much art as you can. Find out what it is that you like or dislike about a piece. Write it down. What you like in other artists' work will reveal important clues to guide you in your own style. Spend time meditating or daydreaming on ways you can use what you have discovered to design your own quilts.

Trying to copy someone else's style never works because it doesn't come from *your* heart. When you are working in another artist's style, your own natural creative ability is stifled. Let it out. There is no right or wrong way to create. Stepping aside and letting go comes with an awareness and trust in yourself and your process.

Take baby steps. Don't critique your efforts as you go. Make something and set it aside. Let it grow on you. Don't compare your beginner's efforts to other artists who have been creating their art for years. Don't start out trying to create a masterpiece—perfection is a creativity killer. Start simple. Remember, this is trial and error. The artists you admire so much go through the same thing every time they make art.

Trust your instincts, not your friends'. Van Gogh never sold a painting while he was alive, but he never gave up working on his own vision. He couldn't. He had to create what was in his heart. Your intuition is a lot smarter than you think. Create based on what you, not others, think.

Trust your own heart. Learn to put your work out in the universe. Some things will be flops, some will be OK. Some will be really good in your eyes and some will be really good in others' eyes.

Don't be afraid to make mistakes. Just create something and go on to the next one. Eventually you will have a body of work that is true and good and comes from your heart. You will have found your own style.

originality is the unsought and unnoticed product of a gifted artist, a successful attempt to be honest and truthful. The deliberate search for a personal style inevitably interferes with the validity of the work because it introduces an element of arbitrariness into a process that can be governed only by necessity.
Rudolph Arnheim

Trust your own heart. Learn to put your work out in the universe.

Making Room for Making Art

I have six children, four still at home. My husband and I have had our own real estate appraisal business for over twenty years. I returned to college four years ago to complete the undergraduate degree I started 34 years ago, and have been creating, traveling, and teaching art for the past four years. The point is, if I can fit art into my life, I bet you can, too.

After many busy but unhappy years spent not creating art because I didn't have time, I came to the realization that making art made me happy and that my happiness was dependent upon my finding a way to fit art into my life. Discovering how to do this didn't come all at once, but I can tell you when it began.

whatever you can do, or dream you can do, begin it. Boldness has genius, power and magic in it.

Goethe

HOW TO FIT ART INTO YOUR LIFE

I was taking an evening class on Unlocking Creativity. The homework assignment was to turn a negative into a positive. The negative was obvious—NO TIME. But how could I turn that into something positive? I knew I was going to have to find time, even make time. Instead of wishing my time away, I decided to take every five or ten minutes of free time I had and do something art-wise. I wanted to see how much art time I could actually find in a week. I recorded those minutes on blocks of wood left over from the ongoing renovation of our house. Blocks of Time!

At the next class I presented the teacher with a box full of my blocks of time. I had accumulated over eight hours of art time. My little blocks of time added up. The secret is in the piecing together of seemingly disparate blocks to create a wondrous whole—as with making a quilt!

This is a mystical path. You walk on it daily without knowing what will come tomorrow. But you trust, by writing down the daily fragments of awareness, that a larger network will gradually emerge, that images will come forth, a theme or direction may appear, all of which you could never have outlined, but which emerge out of deep necessities within us.

Burghild Nina Holzer

Small projects, like the ones in this book, lend themselves to working in small blocks of time and keep the flow going. The key is to be ready to create art on a moment's notice and to do the kind of art that lends itself to spontaneity.

For all of us, the key is to pay close attention to which activities make us feel most alive and in love with life— and then try to spend as much time as possible engaged in those activities.

Nathaniel Branden, Ph.D

Start and the Art Will Follow

Keep your art supplies together—Don't waste time assembling and searching.

Immediate gratification—Work on something that gives quick results so you will be eager to continue.

Choose an art form with little prep time—If you have to clear a space, pull out a lot of materials, set up a lot of things, you run out of time.

Trick yourself—If you are too tired to work on art, tell yourself you'll just fool with your art supplies for *just five minutes*. Chances are you'll get hooked and end up working much longer.

Keep many projects going—Different projects call for different tasks at different times. If there's always something to work on, you can fit it in.

Leave it out—Don't put your project away. Find a place to leave it where you can see it. It will serve as a reminder—and be easy to pick up and work on later.

A day to start—OK, you do need a big block of time to get the ball rolling. Gather all your supplies and materials beforehand. Everyone can find one day to devote to themselves, so do it. Use it to get started on a project or two. Decide what you want to do and start. This is the beginning of your adventure.

Someone to share it with—There's nothing like an understanding friend to keep you motivated. Don't know anyone? Go to a local Art League or quilt guild meeting, take a class, get online. My best supporters are people I met on the Internet.

Always leave something to do—If you finish a project in your block of time, you will have to face the hurdle of starting another. The temptation is to put it off and not start. Starting something is the hardest part. Begin thinking about it as you approach the end of a project. Leave the last bit for the next time so that you will be eager to return to it, then finish it quickly enough to start something new.

Take advantage of other time—Use the time you spend driving, cooking, doing laundry, etc., to design and dream up new ideas so that when your hands are free and you're home you can dive right in.

Work where you spend time—It takes effort and discipline to go to a separate room (usually one you rarely go in). If your work is where you spend most of your time, it's easier to work on it in your spare moments.

Don't judge, and don't give up—Somewhere along the way you will think your work is no good and wonder why you are even bothering. This is the time to persevere! Even the most accomplished, full-time artists feel that way; but they work through it because they know it is common and temporary. Don't give up!

Fill your head—Read, look at art books and magazines. Fill your head with inspiration so that when you have the time to create, you have the desire and ideas. If your head and heart are filled with art, it will eventually burst out into your creations.

Find your art—If you are not having fun, it isn't the right thing to be doing. Stressing out over your art is not the idea. If you're not enjoying what you're doing, perhaps it is too hard, too serious, too intricate for your time or temperament. Try something else.

Go to bed happy—During the week, my free time usually comes at 9 or 10 pm. Yes, I'm exhausted, but I drag myself over to my work and get going. I work, I get energized, and then I fall into bed exhausted and happy. I don't have to go to bed feeling disappointed or down on myself for being lazy or not pursuing my dreams.

Don't wait—Waiting until you know all the answers is just another form of procrastination. Too many people waste time thinking they will start "just as soon as I learn one more thing" and continually take classes or read how-to books without ever trying anything on their own. Stop reading, planning, and waiting. Dive in!

Nothing looks good—We aren't born artists, just like we aren't born knowing how to read or do surgery or drive a car. It takes practice and hard work. If you work at it, you will eventually create some good stuff.

Trust your intuition—Creating is an innate ability, something we are all born with. Just watch a toddler "make stuff." Part of an artist's talent is trusting your own vision, listening to your own intuition. Always work from the heart.

Steer clear of naysayers—Don't listen to or spend time with people who don't understand or appreciate why you would rather work on your art than go shopping or to a movie. Especially avoid people who put you down or make you feel inadequate.

Fear in sheep's clothing—You may procrastinate, you may say you have no time, but perhaps the problem is that you are afraid that if you try, you will fail. Maybe you think you won't be good enough. The difference between those who fail and those who succeed is that the successful work through their fear. Their desire to create is stronger than their fear of failure.

Create art vs. make stuff—Take the seriousness out of it. Just go play and make stuff. You will be less inclined to criticize your efforts and enjoy the time more if it's play.

1440 minutes—There are 1440 minutes in the day. You can find some of them to devote to your art. Get off the computer, skip the newspaper, clean less, turn off the TV, and get off the phone.

Visual Journals

There's a point in the process of artmaking where every-thing makes sense and just flows. Being "in the flow" is one way of describing that magical state where you are immersed in the act of creating. Staying in flow is one of the most important things for an artist with limited time. If you keep your eye trained and your creative fire always burning, you are able to create on a moment's notice when a block of time opens up for you.

How do you stay in the flow when your time to create is limited? One of the standard methods many artists use to develop and improve their skills is to keep a sketchbook. Maybe you are put off by the word sketchbook because it con-jures up a book filled with actual drawings, and you don't draw. How about keeping a visual journal?

A visual journal is a collection place for things that stim-ulate your creativity. As a fabric artist, I use my journal to create vignettes of color and image that inspire and preserve the myriad ideas and visions that flash by me in and out of the studio.

My pages include quotes or words that inspire, color com-binations that catch my eye when they haphazardly appear in my fabric pile, and collages of leftover scraps from a just-completed project.

My visual journal is a safe and easy space to play and experiment with color combinations and ideas, and a relax-ing activity when I can't find the time or energy to do anything else. It not only provides a source of creative inspi-ration but it keeps the creative flow going in my "off" days. I make sure I can play at a moment's notice by keeping a bag of fabric scraps, a bottle of glue, and my journal within easy reach.

PACK UP YOUR OLD KIT BAG
A Recipe to Facilitate Spontaneous Creating

INGREDIENTS
- Assorted trinkets*
- Craft glue
- Fabric
- Gallon-size resealable bag
- Decorative papers
- Photocopies
- Scissors
- Spiral-bound journal

1. Fill resealable bag with a variety of fabric and paper scraps cut into manageable sizes.

2. Add several photocopies or photos printed on fabric.

3. Insert small bottle of craft glue and one pair of scissors.

4. Mix with spiral-bound journal.

5. Combine ingredients and arrange selected pieces on journal page in an eye-pleasing arrangement. Spread a thin layer of craft glue and adhere items.

6. Garnish, if desired, with treasured trinkets.

7. Repeat Steps 5 and 6 until journal is well done.

*SUGGESTED TRINKETS: buttons, beads, bottlecaps, tags, artificial flowers, ribbons, trims, charms, sequins, found objects, keys, toys, twigs, stones, washers, nails, any-thing small and relatively flat.

where to Find Fabric

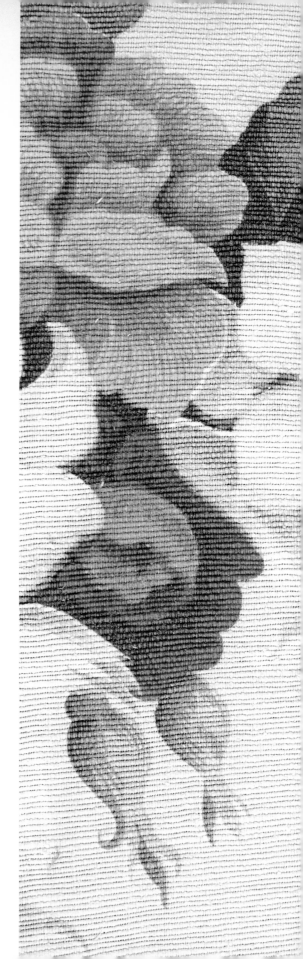

Fabric is everywhere. The easiest place to look is in your closet. Chances are you have clothes that you haven't worn in years. One reason you bought them was because you liked the fabric. Are you brave enough to cut them up? Don't overlook household textiles either. Old cloth napkins, slipcovers, and curtains yield a variety of textures and large-scale patterns.

If your closet didn't yield much in the way of fabric, try someone else's. At estate sales, tag sales, and yard sales, you will often find a variety of textures and patterns and often some vintage fabrics and laces. I love vintage textiles and lace, but they are often expensive to buy. The secret is to buy damaged pieces. Collectors prize pieces in good condition, but magpies like you and me can use the damaged and neglected. It's much easier and prudent to cut into damaged vintage textiles and give them new life than to destroy the integrity of a significant treasure.

Over the years, I have found some lovely old pieces of lace, Victorian cuffs and collars, embroidery, and needlework. For the longest time they sat in a drawer, too precious to use. At least that's what I used to think. Now I employ them as focal points or as eye-catching backdrops in my collage quilts. They aren't doing anyone any good closed away in a box or drawer. If you use them, I can guarantee more will come your way! Another option is to scan them and print them onto inkjet-prepared fabric. Just think of the possibilities!

The next place to find fabric is in a fabric store. It can be an overwhelming experience, even for a seasoned pro like me. I have a simple rule: I only buy what I truly love, and I let price tell me how much to buy. Some stores will cut as little as ⅛ yard and most have ¼ yard minimums. Many stores have a bin of fat quarters of quilting cottons, which is a yard of 45" wide fabric cut into four pieces measuring 18" x 22". They are often more practical than a ¼ yard length that is 9" x 45".

Decorator fabric comes on 60" bolts and is usually more expensive than quilting cottons, but ⅛ yard of 60" fabric goes a long way on small collage quilts. I find most of my decorator fabrics on the remnant table, and I buy the "good stuff" when I have extra money to spend or there is a sale at the store. I add beautiful silks and brocades to my stash because a piece of luxury fabric in a collage of homespun cottons can be the unexpected touch that makes the quilt sing.

At high-end decorators, mill outlets, and everything in between, you can find anything from expensive imported silks to free sample swatches. When you are working small, even the cuttings on the upholsterer's floor are enough to add the magic. Many stores that specialize in decorator fabric sell (or even give away) discontinued samples and remnants. Ask them to give you a call the next time they have some available.

Every once in a while I shop in my pajamas. The Internet has many online fabric stores. The minimum cut online is usually one yard, but just like in the fabric store, many online stores sell fat quarters in a bundled package of coordinated colors and patterns. These already-matched fabrics are a good beginning for a project, but will need to be jazzed up with other fabrics in a variety of weights and textures, like the ones you find in your closet or at the decorating store.

HOW TO INCREASE YOUR STASH

People who accumulate fabric call it their fabric stash. The definition of stash is "a secret place where something is hidden or stored." Well it's no secret in my house! It's everywhere! There's nothing better for inspiration than just the right fabric.

But what do you do when the right fabric isn't a part of your collection? You make it! Building a good fabric stash is fun but expensive, and it can take years. There are many ways to multiply your choices that are easy and inexpensive.

Pleasure is very seldom found where it is sought. Our brightest blazes are commonly kindled by unexpected sparks.

Samuel Johnson

Creativity comes from looking for the unexpected and stepping outside your own experience.

Masaru Ibuka

We live in a web of ideas, a fabric of our own making.

Joseph Chilton Pearce

COLORING FABRIC

Overdyeing

One way to pull a coordinated palette of fabric together is to overdye different fabrics in the same color. Besides coordinating different colors, the main advantage to overdyeing is that the fiber reactive dyes that are used are transparent, so the original pattern on the fabric is not lost. There are many excellent resources on fabric dyeing and many varieties of dyes and methods. The Internet also provides instruction as well as dyers' lists that have ongoing discussions on methods and materials. Cotton and other natural fibers are the easiest to overdye. Synthetics require special dyes and will not absorb dye from the overdyeing process. Blends will react differently to the dye process, depending on the amount of natural fibers, which could be a bonus if you like surprises.

My overdyeing experience has been with fiber-reactive dyes. I use a low-water immersion process that simplifies some of the steps and work in the dyeing process. Even so, the process takes more time, materials, and preparation than I can afford to spend. Nevertheless, the end results are well worth the effort. If you'd like to try your hand at it, please refer to the Resources on pages 126–127 for more information on the use of dyes.

Painting

One of the simplest methods I have found to add color to fabric is to use acrylic paint or ink, not dye. Using paint or ink eliminates the many steps and ingredients that are needed for dyeing, and allows for more spontaneous creating. There are several brands of highly pigmented liquid paints available and most will work on both natural and synthetic fabrics. Transparent liquid acrylic paints can be used to "overdye" commercial fabric or to create your own hand-dyed-looking fabrics. The results will vary depending on the type of fabric to which they are applied. Use opaque paints to add additional color and pattern over transparent paints.

Fluid acrylics are highly pigmented paints in a liquid form that behave like dye. Prewetting the fabric with water and

I never met a color I didn't like.
Dale Chihuly

Tip

While quilted art is not intended to be washed, many of the paints and dyes are designed to be permanent after heat-setting. Read manufacturers' instructions and visit their Web sites for complete instructions and information.

using transparent colors in place of fiber-reactive dyes produces results similar to overdyeing. The color can be applied from gradations of dark to light, depending on the amount of water used. It can be applied to wet or dry fabric and thinned with water once it is on the fabric—or mixed with water prior to painting, depending on the desired results. There are mediums you can add that help the paint penetrate the fabric, but I get the results I desire without any additives. While your collage quilts will probably never be washed, there are also mediums that stabilize the paints for repeated washings.

When I work with fluid acrylics, I start by squirting a small amount of paint onto the fabric directly from the bottle, then blending it out with a brush. Sometimes I wet the fabric first; however, many times I work directly on dry fabric, then blend it out with a wet foam brush. I like the variation from deep rich color to pale washes.

Another method to add color to small pieces of fabric is to mix a small amount of the fluid acrylic in a cup with a small amount of water—just enough to scrunch the fabric into. There should be just enough paint and water mixture for the fabric to absorb. Turn the scrunched fabric around in the cup until all the paint and water is absorbed. This will create a mottled, uneven color.

Fluid acrylics is concentrated liquid color that will spread to create an even application of color when applied to fabric. Gradations of color are not possible with fluid acrylics, but they can be mixed prior to application—or allowed to mix and flow into each other on the fabric to create subtle color variations. To control color application, paint one area of color, then dry before adding the next color.

Acrylic inks also can be used to color fabric. There are many brands available. Ink comes in small quantities, but it is very concentrated and can be thinned with water. Inks are good for adding color to small areas.

From top:
1. Fluid acrylic on black and white cotton
2. Fiber-reactive dye on barkcloth
3. Acrylic paint stencil on fluid acrylic painted cotton
4. Fluid acrylic on black and white silk

Everyone knows that yellow, orange, and red suggest ideas of joy and plenty.
Eugene Delacroix

Start with White

Adding color to white or off-white fabric can give you a range of colored fabrics. These fabrics can then serve as a background for your own pattern application. The coloring I do is intended to create small one-of-a-kind pieces of fabric to use in a collage quilt. These special pieces of fabric that you create serve to make your work unique and add the personal touch that can set your work apart.

Different weights and fibers will react differently to the paint or dye and the resulting color vibrancy. There are endless combinations of paint, dye, and fabric. I approach coloring fabric with a "let's see what happens" outlook and work with whatever I get. If my end result doesn't work in the project I have in mind, it goes into my collection of one-of-a-kind fabrics until it finds a home in another project.

I generally start with anywhere from an 8" square to a fat quarter of bleached white muslin or cotton duck. Paint color on directly or submerge the fabric in a paint-and-water mixture. Different effects can be achieved, depending on whether you begin with wet or dry fabric. If you start with wet fabric, the color will move on its own across the fabric until the pigment is absorbed. The wetter the fabric is, the more the color will spread. Working with two or more colors on wet fabric will allow the colors to run into each other and create even more colors. I prefer this "work-in-the-moment" approach, knowing that these are one-of-a-kind results that can never be reproduced again. It keeps the work fresh.

Working on dry fabric will give you sharper edges and more control in color placement and saturation. To prevent colors from blending, dry the fabric with an iron or blow-dryer before adding the next color. Acrylic paints and inks can be ironed dry with a layer of waxed paper between the fabric and iron to keep the iron clean. Thick applications of paint are best air-dried or speeded along with a blow-dryer.

Tricks with Black (and other shady colors)

Black and other dark fabrics are great for both adding and subtracting color.

Fulvia Luciano applies pattern to white fabric with paint, crayons, dye, stamp ink, and watercolor pencils (see Love you, mean it quilt on pages 86-87).

Adding Color

Adding color to black or other dark fabrics requires the use of opaque paints. Opaque paints that can be used directly from the bottle, thinned with water or mixed with mediums to make them suitable for screen-printing or other applications.

Opaque paints are thicker than most translucent paints and inks, and they may change the hand of the fabric. This is usually not a concern when the fabric you are painting is going to end up in a collage. Hand-stitching may be more difficult through heavy applications of opaque paint, but there is seldom a problem with machine-stitching.

Subtracting Color

Another way to create pattern on dark fabrics, especially black fabric, is to subtract color with bleach. The fabric must be one of the natural plant fibers: cotton, linen, or rayon. Bleach will disintegrate wool and silk fibers and it will not react on synthetics. Blends may or may not react, depending on fiber content. Bleach can be used in any patterning process that paint and ink can—as along as you are working on cotton, linen, or rayon.

The easiest way to test fiber content is to cut a 1" square of fabric and place it on a disposable surface: paper plate, margarine tub, etc. Pour one teaspoon of straight bleach on the fabric. Changes should begin to occur in about two minutes. If nothing has happened after eight minutes, then it is most likely made of synthetic fibers and will not react to bleach. If the fibers are brittle and pull apart easily afterward, they may be animal fiber or simply not suitable for bleaching.

Black is created by mixing several colors of dye together. When you apply bleach to black fabric the results can be surprising. You may see colors ranging from blue to red and shades from brown to pink. There is no way to know what colors will be revealed beforehand. The color appears in varying hues, depending on how long the bleach is left on the fabric. In most cases, the longer you leave the bleach on, the closer you will get to white. By watching the bleaching process, which can take anywhere from two to eight minutes, depending on the dyes and the bleach solution, you can stop

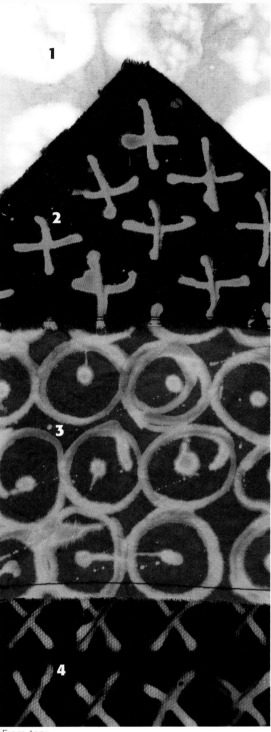

From top:
1. Stamping with bleach
2. Bleach pen on black cotton
3. Bleach pen on blue cotton
4. Bleach pen on black cotton duck

the bleaching when you see a color you like. Remember that the fabric will be lighter when dry.

Use a mixture of bleach and warm water. Start with a ratio of five parts water to one part bleach (5:1), again testing on a 1" square. You can use stronger solutions, but don't exceed a 1:1 ratio of bleach to water. If you are going to spray the bleach, a 1:1 ratio is preferable.

To stop the action of the bleach, soak the fabric in a neutralizing solution of one part vinegar to three parts water for a few minutes. Rinse the fabric in cold water and wash with dish or laundry detergent. Bleach left in fabric will disintegrate the fibers over time.

There are two products now available that make the bleaching process easier: 1) a bleach pen, 2) gel cleansers with bleach. Both come ready to apply and result in similar effects. Drawing lines and discharging with stencils and stamps is much easier with this thickened bleach and pattern is easier to control.

PATTERNING FABRIC

Art is pattern informed by sensibility.
Herbert Read

Another way to multiply your fabric stash or create fabric for a specific quilt is to add pattern to existing solid color fabric, or even to commercial fabric that already has a pattern. Patterning fabric can be as simple as drawing lines with a permanent marker or bleach pen, or as complex as silkscreening. Tools and techniques include rubber stamps, brushes, stencils, toothbrush spattering, spraying or block printing. There are many excellent books, magazines and online resources that provide instruction and ideas. Several methods can be combined on one piece to produce a rich, multilayered surface.

The patterning you add can be an integral part of your finished quilt (see quilts by Fulvia Luciano on page 87, Lisa Engelbrecht on page 67 and Rayna Gilman on page 93), or serve as a backdrop for your central collage (see Writer's Block on page 89 and The Artist in Me on page 101).

Left side: unbleached cottons
Right side: after bleaching

BLEACHING TIPS

- Before beginning, read and follow the safety information on the bleach bottle.

- Always use fresh bleach. Bleach is inexpensive and old bleach does not discharge as quickly.

- Mix bleach with warm water. Cold solutions do not discharge as quickly as warm ones.

- Wear old clothes. Splashes can occur.

- Wear protective gloves. Bleach is not kind to your skin.

- Work in a well-ventilated area, near an open window, or outdoors.

- If spraying or misting bleach, wear a protective mask and protect work area from overspray.

- Prewashing your fabric is optional. You may get different results, depending on any finishes that may be applied to the fabric.

HOUSEHOLD ITEMS FOR STAMPING

- kitchen utensils
- screening
- nonslip rug pads
- sponges
- corrugated cardboard
- wooden blocks
- bottlecaps
- carved vegetables
- thread spools
- dried pasta
- leaves
- cardboard shapes
- paper clips
- corks
- any tool you can put paint on

Stamping

Fluid acrylics, pearlescent paint, and Tsukineko All Purpose Ink as well as other craft and fabric paints can be used to stamp on fabric. There are also rubber stamp ink pads that are suitable for stamping on fabric.

You can stamp onto any fabric; however, smooth, tightly woven fabrics give the best results. Prewashing is recommended but is not always possible, nor is it necessary since you will not wash your collage quilt. Moreover, the possibility of the paint separating or washing out of the fabric surface is almost nil. Stamping on sheer fabrics produces fabrics that allow for wonderful layering techniques. Be sure to protect the surface beneath the fabric as paints will seep through to whatever is underneath.

Choose stamps with well-defined lines and large patterns. Fine detail does not translate well onto a fabric surface. You can also use items from around the house to stamp patterns onto your fabric.

Create homemade stamp pads, using a felt pad. Cut the felt to the size of your largest stamp. Wet the felt with water and squeeze dry. Place the pad on a disposable, nonabsorbent surface like aluminum foil or waxed paper. Pour any water-based paint or ink to saturate the felt. Pour a small amount of paint or ink onto a disposable surface and use a foam brush to apply one or more colors to the stamp. Note: To keep the pad moist between uses, seal in a plastic bag.

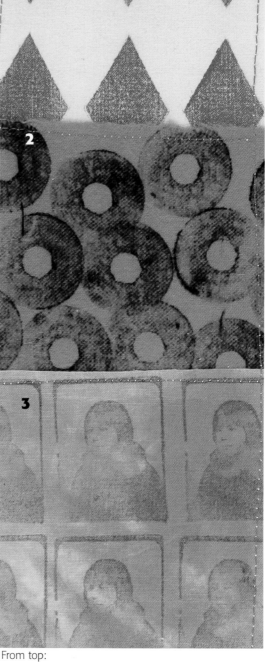

From top:
1. Fabric stamped with foam stamp
2. Fabric stamped with thread spool
3. Fabric stamped with rubber stamp

Another option is to carve your own stamps. Creating your own stamps is fairly easy and can be done almost anywhere: in the car, at a sports game, or in front of the TV. It's a good on-the-go activity and a great way to build up a very personal artistic collection. Be the envy of all your friends!

Carve temporary stamps from fruits and vegetables, like apples and potatoes. Make permanent stamps from erasers and other soft carving blocks. There are eraser-like materials that come in various sizes available as well. You can even carve a 9" x 12" stamp.

You will need some carving tools. A basic linoleum cutter set provides everything you need. Use craft knifes and objects from around the house to create holes and shapes in the carving block.

Draw simple shapes and designs right onto the eraser or carving block with a pencil or ballpoint pen. More complex designs can be transferred to the stamp surface by making a photocopy (not inkjet). Transfer it to the stamp surface by placing it face down and burnishing the copy with a cotton ball and acetone (nail polish remover) or solvent (see Toner Transfers on page 50). Remember that all designs will be reversed, so if you have lettering or designs that have specific orientation, you will need to make a mirror-image copy before transferring it to the stamp.

Stenciling: Positive and Negative

A variety of stencils can be purchased at craft stores. There are many options and designs available: large wall stencils, small stencils designed for fingernail and body art, and small brass and plastic stencils for general craft uses. On small stencils, you can use a small ink pad or small stencil brushes with some of the thicker paints.

Simple stencils also can be made from adhesive or contact paper. You double your patterning options because you will have both a positive and a negative to work with after you cut the design from the contact paper. Draw designs or shapes onto contact paper. Cut with a craft knife or scissors. Remove backing paper and apply adhesive side of shape to fabric.

Background fabric stamped with hand-carved stamp

TIPS FOR FABRIC STAMPING

- Use stamps with well-defined lines and high relief.
- Work on a protected surface. Paint and ink may seep through fabric.
- Stamp on a firm, smooth, slightly padded surface. Felt or newspaper make good padding.
- Smooth, high-thread-count fabrics produce clearer images than textured ones or fabrics with a large weave.
- Use unscented baby wipes to clean the ink off of your rubber stamps as soon as you finish stamping.
- Press the stamp firmly, but not too hard. You do not want the paint to seep outside of the image area or bleed into the fabric.
- Avoid rocking the stamp while stamping.
- Color-in a stamped image with pencils, fabric markers or small brushes. Make sure all paint/ink is dry before adding another color.

Apply several cut-out shapes to the fabric, creating either an organized or random pattern. Spray or brush paint or bleach gel onto the fabric. The areas where the cut-out shapes are adhered will remain unpainted. On another piece of fabric, you can apply the contact paper that the shape was cut from to produce a positive print. The background fabric will remain the original color this time and paint will only be applied to the cut-out areas.

Painting and Drawing

Why not draw your own designs on fabric? You don't need to be confident with your drawing skills to make marks on your fabric. Simple line drawings can be just as effective and meaningful as drawings by Leonardo da Vinci, if they are made from the heart. Remember, this is background patterning, not your focal point. Swirls, squiggles, Xs, and Os (see Fulvia Luciano's quilt on page 87) are all easy to do. You will see that the more fun you have, the richer your work will be.

There are several permanent marking pens available for drawing and mark-making on fabric. Just be sure that the markers won't bleed if they come into contact with any water-based process you may do after you use them. Even though a marker says it is permanent, it may require heat-setting or a curing period before you can wet the area. Test on scrap fabric by making a few marks with the pen or marker. Wet the fabric. If the ink does not run, it's safe to use. If the ink runs, try again, but heat-set the inks by ironing with a very hot, dry iron before wetting again.

Drawing or mark-making with paintbrushes will give a softer line with softer edges. Use any of the paints and inks that have been mentioned before. A variety of results are possible, depending on how much water is in the brush, how wet or dry the fabric is, and how thick the paint is. Remember to dry the fabric between paint applications if you don't want colors bleeding into one another. Use a wide paintbrush to draw wide columns of color, a thinner one for more delicate lines. Experiment, play, see what you can come up with. Don't think of this as the endpoint of the quilt; it's only the beginning.

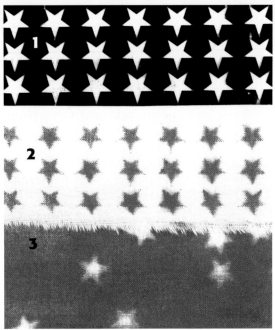

From top:
1. Stencil from adhesive star sheet
2. Stars stencilled on white cotton
3. Adhesive stars adhered to white fabric
   Fabric colored with fluid acrylic paint

Painting is easy when you don't know how, but very difficult when you do.
Edgar Degas

Screening

You're probably familiar with the term silk screen. Silk-screening, however, is only one method of screen-printing. The screening process is more labor intensive due to the time and materials involved in the preparation of the screens. Screen-printing is similar to printing with stencils; however, it has the advantage of being a faster and more efficient way for repeated printing of a design, particularly on several large pieces of fabric. Screen-printing is also used to print successive applications of color to a design where accurate registration is necessary.

Screen-printing is done by pulling paint or thickened inks or dyes across a fine mesh screen that has some areas blocked to prevent the paint from going through, resulting in a pattern on the surface beneath the screen. Blocking areas of the screen works in much the same way as stencils do and can be done using a variety of materials such as paper, wax, and photo emulsion. If you are interested in experimenting with screen-printing, there are numerous sources of information and instruction, both in print and on the Internet.

In her quilt (see Time & Again on page 93), Rayna Gilman has used thermal screen-printing to print images of an old factory building and a gentleman from an old cabinet photo. Thermal screen-printing screens are created from mimeograph machines, a printing technology used before photo-copy machines. Thermal screen-printing uses a photo-copy (not inkjet) to create a screen. The copy can be of anything, from original drawings to copyright-free clipart. It provides very detailed photo screens and is great for making repeated prints from a favorite photograph. The machines (no longer manufactured) are expensive and hard to come by. However, there are cost-effective sources that will make thermal screen-printing screens from your copies (see Resources on page 126–127).

Unexposed screen

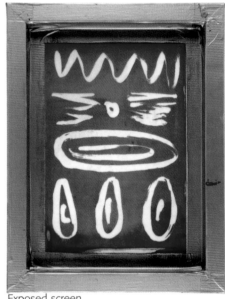
Exposed screen

Inexpensive home-made screens by Christine Adams

Photos on Fabric

There are several ways to get your photos onto fabric. All of the photos on the quilts in *Quilted Memories* have been transferred to fabric, using transfers, computer printing, or photocopy technology. Each method has its own unique look, and the transfer method you choose can work to your artistic advantage and complement the overall design and message of the quilt.

I know with certainty that a man's work is nothing but the slow trek to rediscover, through the detours of art, those two or three great and simple images in whose presence his heart first opened.

Albert Camus

Photography is a small voice, at best, but sometimes one photograph, or a group of them, can lure our sense of awareness.

Eugene Smith

Photo printed directly on fabric

The Photos

One of the questions I am asked most frequently is, "Where do you get your photos?" Just like my fabric collection, my photo collection has been years in the making. After sifting through family photographs, I set my sights on local estate sales, postcard shows and antique shops. However, just like a lot of things, the Internet has changed the way I now find most of my photos. If a picture is worth a thousand words, it's also worth a few dollars to me. I find everything from abandoned family snapshots to vintage postcards and cabinet photos. The one thing I make certain to do is to buy photographs and images that are copyright-free or copyright-expired.

Other image sources include: clipart books with copyright-free images, stock photo houses that sell images; CDs available for purchase with photo collections compiled for artists; copyright-free images from the Library of Congress; and the most obvious source, your own photographs. If it's a vintage look you're after, there are software programs and printers that convert your digital or scanned images into sepia-like prints, add scalloped borders, or convert color to black-and-white.

TIPS ON COPYRIGHTS

If you create solely for your own eyes and no one will ever see your work, then you probably don't have to worry too much about copyright issues. However, limiting your view as to who will see your art is just as big a mistake as ignoring copyrights. The rule to follow is: When in doubt, do not use. Many artists avoid the issue entirely by only using material that is in the public domain. This includes work for which the copyright has expired, not been renewed, or was never granted. The following information is taken from the US Copyright Office Online Information Center:

"For works first published or copyrighted between January 1, 1923, and December 31, 1949, but not renewed, if no renewal registration was made, copyright protection expires permanently at the end of the 28th year of the year date it was first secured."

You can now search online for copyrights and copyright extensions at the US Copyright Office Web site (see Resources on pages 126–127). A work published before January 1, 1978, and copyrighted within the past 75 years may still be protected by copyright in the United States if a valid renewal registration was made during the 28th year of the first term of the copyright.

Since 1978, all works created are copyrighted from the moment of creation, whether published or not, for a period that extends far beyond our lifetimes.

From Photo To Printer

There are several ways to get your photos into the computer and ready for printing. The most versatile equipment for this is the all-in-one printer/scanner/copier. Place any photo or image on the flatbed and either scan it into the computer or copy it directly onto fabric.

With a scanner, you are able to transfer photos onto your computer, which you can then print out on your inkjet printer. The scanner allows you to crop your photos and adjust their color and resolution. There are also many other software programs that enable you to adjust the resolution, size, and brightness of your original—as well as alter the color—once the photo is on your computer. Such programs often come with the purchase of a digital camera. If you do not have photo-editing software, you can still adjust the color, saturation, and tone of your photos on your computer by using the "Properties" tab found in the print menu when you click on "Print."

Even if you do not have photo-editing software, you can print a full page of photos that have been saved to your computer by creating a document with your word processing software and printing from that. See your word processing software manual to learn how to add photos to documents.

Many times you will want to print your photos or text in reverse, or mirror-image, for making transfers. You will find these and other printing options once you send the page to the printer. When you click on "Print," the print menu appears and you will see the "Properties" tab. When you click on "Properties," another box will open. The names will vary depending on your printer, but look for the box that says "Mirror-Image" or "Flip," or something similar. Check the box that applies and the page will be printed in reverse, ready for transferring.

If you have one of the newer digital cameras, there are now many compatible printers that allow you to insert the camera disk into the printer and print your photos without a computer. Some of the printers only print individual 4" x 6" photos. Inkjet-prepared fabric and transfer paper and transparencies can be cut to fit these printers. Many of these are small and lightweight for quilters on the go.

Tip

You can set your scanner to scan at high or low resolution. A resolution of 200 to 300 dpi (dots per inch) is sufficient for printing onto most fabrics. If you want to enlarge a small photo, set the scanner resolution higher (no larger than 600 dpi) to retain accurate color and detail. Some older computers may not be able to handle large files; if your computer won't (or can't) work with a large resolution file, then you will need to work with smaller files (lower dpi or smaller image size) or upgrade to a new computer.

Tip

It's cheaper to print on paper while fine-tuning your photo's color adjustments and size. Keep in mind that photos printed on paper will appear brighter than photos printed on fabric, due to the fact that fabric absorbs ink differently than paper.

Direct Printing On Fabric

When I first started making quilts with photo imagery, I had to do a lot of planning and make a trip to the copy shop every time I wanted another photo on fabric. This was before the days of personal computers and affordable color printers. It was not the ideal situation for someone with limited time who craved spontaneous creativity. I had to gather all my photos and copyright-free images together, sometimes making several prior trips to the copy shop for color enlargements or reductions. After all of my images were attached to an 8½" x 11" sheet of paper, and my fabric was cut to size, off I would go to the one copy shop in town that offered to print photos onto fabric. (It was a popular hangout for local quilters.)

Copies were made onto a transfer paper that was then bonded to my fabric on a heat press. The resulting transferred image felt rubbery and changed the hand of the fabric. It was expensive, time consuming, and often disappointing to make a copy of a copy and lose color quality and definition. The day I got my first color inkjet printer was not only one of the happiest days in my art life, it also opened the gates to a flood of inspiration, experimentation, and possibilities that shows no signs of dwindling. Above all, it allowed for spontaneity.

Right from the start, I knew I would be printing many photos on fabric. I prepared my own fabric with Bubble Jet Set, a solution that makes the inkjet printer ink permanent on fabric. There is a lot of preparation involved, but it is still the most economical way to prepare fabric for inkjet printing. Also, with Bubble Jet Set you can prepare any type and color of fabric for inkjet printing, whereas most commercially prepared fabric only comes in cotton. There are a few sources that sell a variety of silks and other fabric, but they only come in white. White fabric is usually preferred because the printed colors will be true. Photos and images printed on other colors will be darker and will vary from your original, but the look can be an effective and artistic addition to your quilt design.

PREPARING YOUR OWN FABRIC FOR INKJET PRINTING

Currently the only product available for preparing your own fabric for inkjet printing is Bubble Jet Set (see Resources page 126).

- Cut your fabric to a size slightly larger than your printer will accept (usually 9" x 12")
- Soak one or several pieces of fabric in enough BJS solution to cover fabric for five minutes.
- Hang or lay flat to dry.
- Iron out any wrinkles and iron fabric to a backing (freezer paper, fusible web, or a full-size adhesive label) so it will go through your printer.
- Trim to 8" x 11".
- Print photo using inkjet printer.
- Rinse fabric to remove excess ink.

Because I have done so much printing on fabric over the years, I decided to reward myself by using commercially prepared fabric. Printing on fabric is more fun than preparing fabric to print on! I buy pretreated, paper-backed fabric on large rolls and cut it to size to keep my cost down. It's possible to buy fabric for inkjet printing in several quantities, from packages of six precut/prebacked sheets to large rolls (see Resources on page 126). When buying, make your decision based on how much printing you plan to do.

Inkjet Printing on Fabric: Answers to Commonly Asked Questions

Gloria Hansen

For printing on fabric, what are the advantages and disadvantages of dye-based and pigment-based inkjet ink?

The advantages of dye-based inks are that they are less expensive to produce and are considered by many to have a wider color gamut. The colorant is liquid, resulting in the dye penetrating the fibers of the fabric. Because dye-based inks are water soluble, a disadvantage is that the ink will run when wet. Additionally, they are light sensitive, will fade faster and can have more of a color shift than pigment-based inks.

Pigment-based inks use a solid colorant to achieve color. Once the water in the solution has evaporated, the particles will not go back into solution. They are thus more water-resistant. Even without any type of treatment, there is no immediate color loss if an image gets wet. Additionally, pigment-based inks are much more UV resistant, meaning they will fade far slower in sunlight than dyes. However, because the colorant is solid, the pigment sits on the fibers rather than penetrating them. While the image can be washed, the rubbing together of the fabric onto itself or other fabrics can cause a weathered look.

If you are creating collage quilts or other items that will receive little or no washing, pigment-based inks are recommended.

Is there any way to prevent pigment-based inks from scuffing off the fabric when washed or rubbed against other fabric?

This condition is also called "crocking" or "weathering." The textile industry cures this by applying a binder or sealant to finished products. By the time you read this, there may be products on the market specifically to help greatly reduce, if not prevent, this problem. In the meantime, if this is a concern, experiment by applying a thinned-down acrylic colorless extender to your printed piece. Application can be by spray bottle or by dunking a printed piece of fabric into a watered-down extender solution. Different extenders will produce different results, depending on your printer ink, the fabric you print on, and so forth.

When printing on fabric, is it always necessary to use a pretreated fabric?

If you are using dye-based inks it's necessary, as any water or high humidity can cause the image to run. If you're using a pigment-based ink and are not planning to wash your image, it is not essential. However, it's the union of the treated fabric with the inkjet inks (pigment or dye) that will create a better chemical bond, brighter colors, and ultimately a better and more durable printed image. The most popular do-it-yourself pretreatment is Bubble Jet Set 2000 (see Resources on page 126). Many brands of pretreated fabrics are also available.

How long does the Bubble Jet Set solution last and how quickly should BJS-treated fabric be used?

While unused solution can be poured back into the bottle, users should be aware that once a bottle is opened, there is a shelf life to the product of approximately one year. Jerome Jenkins, developer of Bubble Jet Set, advises, "Once dried, the fabric should be printed on immediately. [If you wait] the solution will oxidize and will not be as effective." While I found little difference between prints done on freshly treated fabric and fabric treated several weeks prior, your results may vary depending on what printer and fabric you use.

What fabric is best to use with Bubble Jet Set or other pretreatments?

I've obtained the best results using natural fabrics marked "PFD"—prepared for dyeing. These fabrics have been desized and "sourced" (washed with industrial detergents). PFD fabric is most receptive to receive ink. There are several excellent mail order sources for PFD fabrics (see Resources on pages 126–127).

You can also print on natural fabrics purchased from your local quilting store. For best results, scour your fabric to remove sizing, waxes, oils, and finishes. Wash by hand or machine in hot water. Add ½ teaspoon of detergent plus ½ teaspoon of soda ash per pound of fabric. Dry and press.

What is the best way to wash fabric with inkjet images printed on them?

If you need to wash inkjet-printed fabrics, washing with a small amount of detergent is recommended. Synthrapol is unique in that it can be used as a prewash to remove impurities from the fabric and help ensure even dyeing—and as an afterwash to remove excess dye. It also helps whites and light colors stay bright, and works to prevent darker dyes from backwashing onto lighter colors. If you don't have Synthrapol, any product with a neutral pH, such as baby wash or a gentle fabric cleaner, is a good choice. Regular fabric washes should be avoided, as they contain optical brighteners that can also be too harsh on inkjet-printed fabrics.

Why is it important to wash the chemical from the image-printed fabric?

Dye-based inkjet printers will always lay down more ink than the fabric can absorb. Thus, it's important to remove the excess dye out of the fabric. If you are using pigment-based inks, the fabric should still at least be dunked in cold water, if even for seconds. This will release the excess chemical in the fabric and neutralize the chemical bonding process.

How can I keep up with new products and trends for inkjet printed fabric?

Printers, ink, media, and chemical formulations are continually evolving and improving while becoming more affordable. What is available today is very different from the products available only three to five years ago. Visit the Web sites of manufacturers to see what new products may help your work or business.

Gloria Hansen is an award-winning quilt artist who began using an inkjet printer to print on fabric in the mid 1990s.

Laser Printers

Photos and text may also be printed on laser (or toner) printers. These copies are also known as photocopies and should not be confused with inkjet prints. Your local copy shop uses black-and-white and color laser printers. The printing process uses static electricity as a temporary glue to bind fine powder toner particles to paper/fabric, and heated rollers to melt and fuse the toner to the paper/fabric. While the inks are fused by the heat of the printer, I find that the inks must have additional heat-setting with a hot, dry iron. A spray of workable fixative will add extra insurance against any smearing. Laser-printed inks will fade with washing, but that should not be a problem in a collage quilt that won't be washed.

Color laser printers are still a bit pricey for home use, but some of you may have a black-and-white laser printer at home. I have one that I use to print quotes on fabric, and occasionally a photo, but I prefer to print even black-and-white photos on my color inkjet printer because they look more like the originals. In order to print on fabric, it must be backed with a support to allow it to go through the printer, usually freezer paper or paper-backed fusible web. Laser printers are very sensitive to fibers and threads, so be sure all loose threads are clipped before printing. I have been printing fabric on my laser printer for years and have not had any printer problems. However, remember that when you use your printer for anything other than the manufacturer-approved media, you do so at your own risk.

TRANSFERRING PHOTOS TO FABRIC

INKJET TRANSFERS

Inkjet transfers are made from photographs and images printed on your inkjet printer. They capture the gentle edges of the costly Polaroid transfer process and the sharpness of direct printing. They allow you to create magical works of art on fabric and paper, and even directly into a journal or altered book. I have always loved the look of transfers but hated the trip to the copy shop for toner copies. I was excited to discover a transfer process that I could do at home using copies made on my inkjet printer.

Tip

Laser/toner photocopies are necessary for some of the techniques used to transfer photos to fabric. Many of the transfer methods for photocopies use unhealthy solvents. Use precautions when working with solvents.

Acrylic Medium Transfers

For fabric transfers, I prefer to use the more liquid matte medium (or fluid matte medium) and transparencies. If you choose to use the paper method, you will need to make the transfer with soft gel medium, as the matte medium is too wet to use with paper. A gel medium transfer sits on the surface of the fabric due to the thickness of the gel, whereas the wetter matte medium penetrates the fabric. The rule is to use gel medium when making transfers from or onto paper.

There are many variables to consider when doing inkjet transfers. I use certain brands because I get consistent results from them. There are many brands of printers and a great variety of inks used, even among different models of the same printer brand. Depending on your printer, your own results may differ. Using a permanent, water- and light-resistant, archival pigment ink is excellent for inkjet transfers. For an in-depth discussion of different printers and inks and specific troubleshooting, join my inkjet transfer Internet discussion group (see Resources on pages 126–127).

As numbered above:
1. Inkjet-transferred from transparency with matte medium onto fabric
2. Inkjet-printed directly on pretreated fabric
3. Copy of original photo inkjet-printed onto photo paper
4. Inkjet-transferred from glossy photo paper with water onto fabric
5. Inkjet-transferred from coated matte paper with acrylic gel medium onto fabric

Acrylic Medium Transfers *continued*

Materials

- Inkjet printer transparency sheets (not quick-drying) and acrylic medium

  OR

- Inkjet imaging photo paper (matte) and soft gel medium
- Inkjet printer
- 1" foam brush
- Copyright-free images
- White or off-white muslin, canvas, duck or any smooth fabric. White gives the best results, but any light-colored, smooth fabric can be used.
- Firm, smooth, water-resistant work surface (wax paper, plastic mat)

Transparency image transferred to fabric with matte medium

Method

1. For transparencies, set printer to the "Transparency" setting and print desired images onto transparency. If using coated photo paper, use plain paper setting. Remember to set printer to print in "Reverse" or "Mirror image" if desired, or if there is text. Print a whole sheet of images at the same time to reduce waste.

2. Cut out image and set next to work area.

3. Brush acrylic medium onto fabric. Different fabrics will soak up more or less medium. You want an even application that feels smooth to the touch. Lightly run your finger over the medium, feeling for very dry or very wet areas. Smooth to an even application large enough for the image. The smoother you get it, the less streaky the transfer will be.

Paper image transferred to fabric with soft gel medium

4. If you printed your image on coated paper, apply some soft gel medium to the image on the paper in addition to the fabric.

5. Check for the inked side of the transparency and lay onto wet surface. The transparency will stick to the surface. If the surface is too wet, it may slide and smear. If using coated paper, just apply the image with medium on it to the fabric, smoothing out the paper from center to edges.

Above: Photo printed on paper before transfer

Left: Paper after transfer has been made

6. Immediately begin to rub the entire surface with your finger, a rounded burnisher, or the back of a spoon, using some pressure. Starting with the face or focal point of your image, work in a circular motion at first, then horizontally and vertically so that you cover all areas. Apply more pressure in some areas to ensure an even transfer, or less in other areas for a softer effect. Lift a corner of the transparency and check to see that everything has transferred to your liking. Continue to rub more, or remove the transfer if you are happy with your results.

Transparency inkjet transfer
Color added with fluid acrylic

Troubleshooting

No transfer or uneven transfers — If there was not enough medium or it was not smooth in certain areas, you may find that these areas do not transfer as well. Practice will solve these problems eventually, but that's what I like about the method—happy accidents: unpredictable results and the timeworn appearance of the transfers.

Streaks — The result of one of two missteps. Either you didn't smooth out the brushstrokes after you applied the medium before making the transfer, or when you burnished, you used too much back-and-forth motion or burnished too hard in the same direction.

Thin White Lines — Usually caused by fabric threads beneath the transfer area. Check to make sure that there are no threads or other things under the fabric that may cause uneven transfers.

Smears — The result of too much medium on the fabric.

Paper Residue — When using the coated paper method, some paper fibers may remain on the fabric surface when you remove the paper. These can be removed by very gently rubbing them with a wet finger, either before or after they dry.

Paper Sticking to Fabric — If you take too long to make the transfer, the medium begins to dry on the paper, and the paper will stick to the fabric or tear away. Working faster will solve this problem.

Green Cast to Image — When you make a transparency transfer, depending on what type of printer you have, the inkjet inks will transfer off the transparency surface at different rates. With some printers, the color green comes off first and creates a green appearance on the transfer. When this occurs, there is usually enough ink on the transparency to make another transfer; simply transfer a second time to get the correct coloring. This does not happen with paper transfers.

Water Transfers

One of the problems with inkjet inks has been that they are not permanent, that they are water soluble. As artists, we can use this to our advantage. A water transfer is easy to do and once the inks are transferred to fabric, they can be sealed with workable fixative.

There is now a permanent, water- and light-resistant, archival pigment ink available on the market. If you have a printer that uses these inks, you can still make water transfers by doing the transfer soon after printing the image, before the ink sets.

Photo reverse-printed onto glossy photo paper

Materials

- Inexpensive glossy photo paper
- Copyright-free images
- White or off-white muslin, canvas, duck, or any smooth fabric. White gives the best results, but any light-colored smooth fabric can be used.
- Fine-mist spray bottle
- Inkjet printer
- Workable fixative spray
- Firm, smooth, water-resistant work surface (waxed paper, plastic mat)

Photo paper after water transfer

Method

1. Print image onto glossy photo paper.

2. Cut out image and set aside.

3. Lightly mist fabric until evenly damp.

4. Hold photo paper upright; spray with an even, light mist.

5. Place photo paper image-side-down and burnish with finger, spoon-back, or burnisher.

6. Lift corner to check and continue to burnish, or remove photo paper.

7. When fabric is dry, spray with workable fixative to set inks.

Water transfer onto white cotton fabric

The world is so full of a number of things, I'm sure we should all be as happy as kings.

Robert Louis Stevenson

King Me (detail). Water-transferred photo
Inks set with workable fixative

TONER TRANSFERS

Toner transfers are done with laser/toner photocopies, not inkjet copies. You can use either color or black-and-white photocopies along with solvents to transfer images from paper to fabric. Because solvents are toxic and have strong odors, work outdoors when possible, or in a well-ventilated space that is separate from the area where you cook. If you are particularly sensitive to hazardous materials, wear a mask and gloves, or stick with inkjet transfers.

Please be aware that recently my students and I have found that some copies made on newer laser machines will not transfer with any solvents. As manufacturers are constantly perfecting their technology to benefit consumers, artists may find that their much-loved techniques no longer work. However, looking for alternative solutions is what being creative is all about.

Materials

- Solvent (acetone, xylene, lacquer thinner, oil of wintergreen)
- Cotton ball or cotton swab
- Photocopies of copyright-free images
- Firm, smooth, disposable work surface (waxed paper, plastic or paper plate)
- White or off-white muslin, canvas, duck, or any smooth fabric. White gives the best results, but any light-colored smooth fabric can be used.

Method

1. Trim any areas of photocopy that you do not want to transfer.
2. Lay fabric out on smooth surface and place photocopy on fabric, right-side down.
3. Wet the cotton ball until moist and use it to burnish and transfer the image. If there is too much solvent, the inks will blur. Reapply solvent as needed until all of the image has transferred. For small images, using a cotton swab moistened with solvent makes a handy burnishing tool.

Black-and-white toner-printed photo transferred with lacquer thinner

Tip

If your image fails to transfer, try another solvent. If ink is difficult to transfer, burnish harder first, then add more solvent.

Single inkjet image transferred from transparency onto paper painted with pearlescent paint. Transferred imaged scanned into computer to create page of four images, which were then transparency-transferred onto fabric. Red lines added with china marker.

Storytelling

My quilts tell a visual story. Each work is a narrative collage of fabric and image—not overly planned or detailed. My emphasis is on the message, the story. They are not story quilts in the manner of Faith Ringgold or Harriett Powers, whose quilts were made to recount specific events, real or imagined. Rather, my quilts are story *suggestions*. I use fabric and photos, trinkets, and "evidence of the day" to preserve intangible moments that are universally understood. A picture of my father or one of my granddaughters in the kitchen is meant to provide the spark that sets off the imagination of viewers and assist them in making the leap to their own memories and designs.

Scrapbook pages, collage, and mixed-media art are often created to be a record of a specific event or person, but they have a universal appeal because we can all relate to the implied story or memory. Photos are the key to memory. They mark a moment in time, and from them spill sights, sounds, smells, and even colors that are locked inside us.

Fabric has that magical power too. We are literally surrounded by it from our first days to our last. It is a part of every memory we hold. I believe that every fabric tells a story. Fabrics can be utilized and combined to suggest story, or to provide visual clues to the imagination. Schoolgirl plaids, rich red damasks, silk, and felt all suggest certain times, places, and circumstances to us. What fabrics hold special meaning for you?

The story is one of the basic tools invented by the human mind, for the purpose of gaining understanding.

Ursula K. LeGuin

Certain images create private little excitements in the mind.

E. L. Doctorow

Exercise

Look through this book and study the fabrics that were used in each quilt. Write down in your journal the ways you think the pattern, color, or fiber of the fabrics used make a significant contribution to the story. Pull out some of your own fabric and, using it as a prompt, write down all the memories that you associate with the fabric.

Words are powerful tools that should not be overlooked. Often, the addition of text or words can jog a memory and help put images into context. I enjoy finding just the right quote or phrase that assists in revealing the significance behind my work. Other items that can be sewn or attached to your quilt also add to your story. Each ornament, curio, or bit of ephemera is another bridge to association that draws viewers into your work.

Color is another element that you can control. Reinforce the mood and message of your quilt by choosing fabrics and embellishments in colors that are commonly associated with certain events, seasons, periods of history, or everyday occurrences like cooking or going to school. There is an entire field of study on the psychology of color: reds excite, blues are cool, orange makes us want to eat fast food (well, that one is debatable!). Color choices create mood and spark memory. Use color to your advantage to provide another element of unity to your quilt and give impact to your story.

If you pay careful attention to all of the elements you use to create your quilt, you'll find that your storytelling comes of its own accord. In working to integrate all of the materials in your quilt—the fabric, photos, colors, and added embellishments—you will invite the viewer to linger and spend time listening to the story you have to tell. That's part of the magic that will make your art successful.

Fourth Generation Quilts the First (detail) by Alan Kelchner

May Queen (detail)

Alternative Techniques

THINKING OUTSIDE THE BOX

What's all this emphasis on thinking outside the box, anyway? Isn't it easier to use tried-and-true methods and get something you know you will like, especially when you don't have a lot of time to play and create? I know, when I have the time to work on my art, I want to get results. I don't want to spend time working on something new, get frustrated, and end up with a wasted afternoon. However, I've found that when I'm always doing the same thing, I'm missing out on one of the best experiences making art has to offer—the joy of discovery.

I had to teach myself to be open to possibilities; and in the process, I rediscovered the value of play. In doing so, I've learned two very valuable lessons:

1. **What you perceive as a mistake is merely an opportunity for a new design solution.**
   It's a little push from the universe to work harder to solve the problem, to think past the obvious and see what else you can come up with. Edison tried over 6,000 times before he came up with the correct solution to invent the lightbulb. I never would have discovered how to transfer inkjet images if I had just thrown my "mistakes" in the trash.

2. **Just because it doesn't look the way you thought it would does not mean it isn't any good.**
   Don't be so critical of your own work. Don't spend time fussing and fretting, just finish and go on to the next project. This was actually a valuable lesson my daughter taught me when she was two years old. I watched her draw (scribble) picture after picture without ever stopping to judge, criticize, or ask my opinion. It was obvious the joy was in the making, not the product. I have realized that with quantity you get quality.

I do my best work and have the most fun when I'm not sure exactly where I'm heading. The process of discovery is exhilarating.
Jill Cohen

Creativity can be described as letting go of certainties.
Gail Sheehy

For the adventurers out there, let this section be a reminder to try some well-loved or new-to-you techniques. For those that haven't ventured very far from the box, here are some fun techniques from my toy box to inspire you to step outside. You may end up not liking the look of some of these techniques, but you'll never know unless you try.

HOW TO MAKE STUFF LOOK OLD

Taking something new and making it look old may seem silly to some. To me, it imbues the object with life, gives it a history, suggests a story. Aging your materials adds an element of time to your work; for your efforts, you're rewarded with a sense of timelessness. These techniques will work on both your fabric and any additional elements you add to your quilt: paper, buttons, knickknacks, etc.

Coffee- and tea-stained and dyed fabrics and tag

Bleach — A quick soak in a 1:1 solution of bleach and water will give your fabric the fading-over-time look of repeated washings.

Coffee-dye and Sprinkle — Use instant coffee to create an overall look of age or random age spots. Soak fabric in a strong mixture of coffee and hot water until the fabric is the color you want.

For selective age spots, sprinkle or selectively place instant coffee granules onto fabric and spritz with water. When wet, the granules will spread to create little circular age spots.

Frayed Edges — I use what many quilters call raw-edge appliqué. I don't turn under or finish the edges of the fabric before stitching it to my quilt. In fact, the more frayed the fabric is, the better. It provides movement, a sense of time, a look of spontaneity.

THE COLORS OF AGE

Tea = tan, orange, or red (depending on brand used)

Coffee = warm browns

Walnut Ink = cool gray-browns

Quinacridone gold = warm golden yellows

Instant Rust and Patinas — Wrap wet fabric around a rusty old piece of metal or copper and wait for the patinas to occur naturally, or you can paint patinas onto fabric and other objects using a two-step process with an antiquing or rusting solution. A base coat of paint with metallic particles is painted onto the fabric, then a solution is applied to create the desired patina. It's an overnight process. It will change the hand of the fabric, but it can still be sewn on your machine (see The Effects of Time on page 75).

Quinacridone Acrylics — Concentrated liquid acrylic paints produce a golden or yellowed aged look on fabric. Apply it to your fabric straight from the bottle and use a brush and water to spread and dilute it across the fabric, or create a paint/water solution and soak fabric for an overall aged look.

Rip/Tear — If it will rip, I prefer to tear my fabric rather than cut it. The edge looks more alive when torn. For fabrics that do not rip, I try to fray the edge by pulling the cut threads.

Sanding — Use rough sandpaper to sand away some of the fibers on your fabric to create the look of wear.

Tea-dye — Brew a pot of very strong tea. For an even tea-dyed look, wet fabric before adding it to the pot. For a mottled look, scrunch up dry fabric and add to pot. Let it sit undisturbed for a while. When the fabric is the color you want, remove and rinse in cold water. Remember that it will dry lighter than it looks when wet.

To create darker areas or random aging, pour hot water over a few tea bags and place wet tea bags directly on fabric.

Walnut Ink — Walnut ink is sold in crystals and used the same way as coffee. You can do spot aging with the crystals, or create an overall blended look by mixing them with water.

OTHER TECHNIQUES IN MY BOX OF TRICKS

Coloring Black-and-White photos — Vintage photographs and images are almost always black-and-white. Add color with colored pencils and set with workable fixative. You'll feel like a kid with a coloring book again; only this time you'll know you have permission to color outside the lines or make the sky pink.

Patinas added to embossed wallpaper

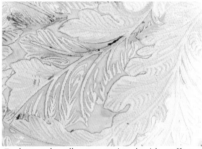
Embossed wallpaper stained with coffee

Mica sewn over photo

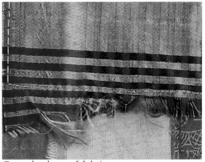
Frayed edges of fabric

Mica — A shiny, transparent, flaky mineral which splits into thin, flat sheets. It is colorless-to-black, and is available in various sizes for craft use. Split off a sheet and stitch it over a photograph to make it look like it is under glass.

Nailheads — Decorative additions to a collage, they come in various sizes and finishes and attach to fabric with a setting tool.

Paper — Treat paper like fabric and sew it into your quilts. Many handmade papers are as strong as fabric. When in doubt, iron paper to fusible web to make it stronger. And don't forget about wallpaper. Embossed wallpaper has a raised-texture that is wonderful to sew and creates magical effects. Remember: paper can take all the dye, paint, and aging techniques that fabric can.

Many kinds of papers are capable of being fed through your printer. Mulberry paper for instance, is excellent for printing and sewing. Paper is also an outstanding surface for transfers, especially handmade and watercolor papers.

Paper ephemera and delicate antique papers can be strengthened with a coat of acrylic gel medium. Apply papers to fabric with more gel medium, or sew them directly onto fabric.

Decorative nailheads added

Sewn card

Original photo

Printed on fabric

Hand-colored with colored pencils

ALTERNATIVE FINISHING TECHNIQUES

Alternatives to Binding — Historically, quilts were bound with a separately attached piece of fabric that served to enclose the batting and neatly finish and protect the edges of the quilt. It had to be easy to remove and replace because the quilt edges became worn with use.

The collage quilts that you create will not suffer from daily use, so a binding no longer serves the same functions as it did in the past. This gives us the freedom to come up with new ways to finish (or not) the edges of a quilt. The quilts in this book show many ideas for decorative and easy quilt finishes.

Fused Strips or Squares — This variation uses a fusible web instead of stitching. Iron fusible web to the back of your chosen binding fabric. Trim edges of finished, but unbound, quilt so they are even. For strips, cut binding fabric to length of four sides of quilt, fold over quilt edges and iron to bond. For a zigzag look, cut enough 1½" squares to go around all four sides of quilt, overlapping. Fold the squares over the edges of the quilt and iron to bond (see Mama with Chickens on page 71, King Me on page 73, Writers Block on page 89).

Package Fold — This is a simple and time-saving method that uses the quilt backing to create a finished edge and border for the quilt. Cut your quilt-backing fabric and batting to the same size as your quilt-collage top—plus enough additional inches on each side to fold over toward front and create a border.

Lay quilt-back fabric right side down. Lay batting on top. Fold two long sides of fabric toward quilt center. Iron. Fold two short sides in the same way you would fold when wrapping a

Pillowcase quilt finish on Spaghetti Sauce

Unfinished fabric edges on Butterfly Girls by Olivia Thomas

Zigzag-sewn and cut edge on Matching Dresses
by Lisa Engelbrecht

Fused-strip edge binding on Mama with Chickens

package, turning the two edges toward the middle at a 45-degree angle. Fold the flap toward the quilt center. Iron. (Trim any bulk that is hidden in the fold.) Lay quilt top on top of folded backing/batting. The quilt top should cover the batting and the folded-in edges of the backing, with the remaining folded backing providing a border for the quilt top. Machine- or hand-stitch around quilt top edge to secure all layers (see Friends on page 63, Leaving Home on page 69, Tender Heart on page 118).

Pillowcase Quilting — The name I give to a technique that provides both a surface for collage and an easy way to finish the edges. So called because you make a pillowcase out of your quilt top, backing fabric, and a layer of batting.

Layer your backing and quilt top, right sides together. Add a layer of thin batting on top of these two fabrics and stitch around the edges, leaving an opening to turn it inside-out. Hand-stitch the opening closed. Collage your fabric, photos and embellishments on the top and machine- or hand-stitch through all layers to create your quilt (see 1924/2004 on page 83, Wings on page 85, Spaghetti Sauce on page 105, May Queen page 107).

Trimmed Felt Edge — Using felt as your quilt batting, let the edges of the felt layer extend beyond the edges of your quilt top and back. Sew around edges of quilt top to secure all layers. Trim felt with rotary cutter using a scalloped or zigzag edge (see School Days on page 99, Waiting (with wings) on page 111).

Unfinished Edges — One option for finishing is not finishing. Simply sew around the raw edges of your fabric to hide the batting and secure layers together (see Butterfly Girls on page 81, Portrait on page 117, Evidence of Family on page 121).

Zig-zag Sewn and Cut Edge — Sew a zigzag stitch around all edges of quilt; trim excess fabric close to outside edge of sewn stitch (see Matching Dresses on page 67, The Effects of Time on page 75, Fourth Generation Quilts the First on page 115).

Detail of package-fold edge finish

Detail showing trimmed felt edge finish

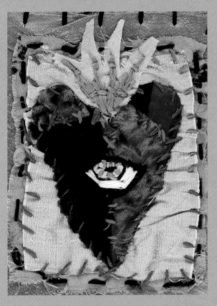

24 *Quilted Memories*

With all of this talk about creating and making quilts and reading about the new techniques and materials you want to try, I bet the ideas are flying through your head. By now, I'm sure you've thought of treasured photos you want to turn into quilted memories and hopefully you have some fabrics, both old and new, to play with. So where do you start? In the next pages you will discover how I, along with twelve other talented artists and quilters, have crafted a memory or keepsake using many of the methods and materials I've shared with you. For some, this was their first attempt at quilting. It was important to me to invite nonquilters to create a quilt for this book because I wanted to show that you don't need any quilting experience to play with fabric and make a wonderful work of art. Whether you have made one quilt or one hundred quilts, you will find a number of innovative techniques and ideas within these projects.

I don't expect you to copy any of these personal quilted memories, nor would I want you to. You have your own memories, photographs, and fabrics that inspire your work. I have presented the steps and in some cases, the inspiration, each quilter used to create her quilt in the hope that their techniques and ideas will help you solve your own technical or creative questions should they arise. I also think it is not only interesting, but informative to see how others tackle a concept from start to finish. Sometimes we get so stuck in our own way of doing things; we miss obvious or innovative solutions. Not only will the next section provide you with visual delight but I am certain you will find it to be a rich source of design, ideas, and inspiration.

Friends

11¾" x 20½"

Friendship is born at that moment when one person says to another: "What! You, too? Thought I was the only one."

C. S. Lewis

True friends are those who really know you but love you anyway.

Edna Buchanan

Being with my friends is like being at a circus. Everything is happening at once. Dressed in our true colors, we show off our own little marvels and amazing art pieces, oohing and aahing, laughing and telling stories. It's a place where I can be silly with people who know and understand me.

In this piece, I made a layered fabric collage with a package fold, all-in-one backing and binding. The clowns were printed on yellow hand-dyed fabric, which I pretreated for inkjet printing. I chose buttons and beads to create a setting for the little antique metal clown figure that reinforces the circus theme.

Materials

- Acrylic gel medium
- Beads
- Buttons
- Colored pencils
- Commercial cotton
- Disposable brush
- Hand-dyed fabric
- Inkjet printer
- Pretreated fabric for inkjet printing
- Quilt batting
- Sari fabric
- Vintage clown diecuts
- Vintage metal clown
- Vintage photo
- Vintage striped cotton duck

Method

1. Scan and print photo and clown diecuts on pretreated fabric.

2. Add color to black-and-white image with colored pencils.

3. Layer selected fabrics, friend photo, and clowns. Stitch together.

4. Cut batting 2½" larger than finished quilt top.

5. Cut backing fabric large enough to fold over batting and under quilt top, allowing enough fabric to fold over and create a 2" border on the front.

6. With right side of backing fabric down, lay the batting onto the backing and fold the edges up around the batting, gift-wrap style. Clip any bulky fabric when folding corners.

7. Pin in place and iron flat.

8. Lay quilt top onto folded backing and batting, right side up.

9. Stitch around the quilt top about ¼" from edge to secure the layers together.

10. Glue metal clown to quilt top with acrylic gel medium. When glue is dry, stitch over clown around neck and arms to secure.

11. Sew beads so that they look like the clown is juggling.

12. Attach large white button to look like clown is balancing on the button, sewing through all layers.

13. Glue vintage metal button inside of white button with acrylic gel medium to give a raised-ball effect.

Watchful Eyes

Lynne Perella
9" x 10¾"

With an eye made quiet by the power of harmony, and the deep power of joy, we see into the life of things.

William Wordsworth

Lynne Perella is a master of mixed-media art who creates richly layered artistic surfaces with the most everyday materials. In Watchful Eyes, she has combined canvas, paper, and fibers to create a unique portrait quilt. The image Lynne chose is from a classic portrait by Ingres that she has admired for years—and often uses in her artwork as a starting point. Like many iconic images, it seems to morph and change, depending on the surrounding elements.

In this case, Lynne wanted to suggest a doll-like figure, overseeing the "real" children below. With the addition of the headdress of fabric, leaves, and twine, and selective stitching details on the face, Lynne dressed up the classic black-and-white portrait image and made it more theatrical. The row of stamped children was imprinted from rubber stamps that Lynne had custom-made from an old family reunion photo in her personal archives.

Materials

- Acrylic gel medium
- Beads
- Cotton fabric
- Cotton lace
- Corrugated papers
- Disposable brush
- Dyed cheesecloth
- Embroidery floss
- Foam-core board
- Hand-dyed silk
- Ink pad
- Polyester batting
- Rubber stamps
- Toner copy of copyright-free portrait
- Twine
- Unstretched canvas
- Metallic thread
- Millinery leaves
- Wooden shadow box

Method

1. Transfer image to canvas (see Toner Transfers, page 50).
2. Stitch canvas onto batting to provide some dimension for further stitching.
3. Stamp family faces onto muslin; tear fabric or trim with pinking shears to size.
4. To add texture, highlight some of the images with small squares of dyed cheesecloth.
5. Use embroidery floss to stitch stamped images onto canvas with a small pillow of batting inserted behind each one.
6. Attach beads randomly over face and background; stitch through all layers.
7. Use embroidery floss to add additional random stitches for texture and highlights.
8. Create headdress using strips of hand-dyed silk, millinery leaves, cheesecloth, twine, cotton lace, and corrugated paper, layering and stitching as you go with an eye for balance.

9. Add additional beads and stitches with metallic threads to complete the vision.
10. Paint and finish shadow box to complement the finished quilt.
11. Back quilted piece with foam-core board and insert into back of shadow box.

Matching Dresses

Lisa Engelbrecht
12" x 12"

A sister is a little bit of childhood that can never be lost.

Marion C. Garretty

You're never fully dressed without a smile.

Martin Charnin

"Every year my mother would dress my sister and I up in matching Easter dresses, which she often sewed herself," says Lisa Engelbrecht. "Now that I am grown, I appreciate the loving care that went into making these outfits, which also included matching headbands and lace anklets." Lisa has commemorated that memory by creating a small embellished quilt that not only frames photographs of those childhood memories, but serves as a canvas for her exquisite calligraphy.

Lisa used a broad-edged calligraphy pen and acrylic inks for the large lettering; a fine-point drawing and illustration pen was used for the smaller script below the names. Similar effects can be achieved by using alphabet rubber stamps and acrylic paint or permanent ink stamp pads. Washes of color over the center portion of the canvas provide the background for the layered collage of photographs, fabric, paper, and charms. A variety of sizes and textures in analogous colors are accented with a punch of rose red. Decorative threads and stitching add the details that pull it all together.

Materials

- Acrylic ink
- Adhesive alphabet stickers
- Assorted buttons
- Assorted fabric scraps for collage
- Backing fabric
- Calligraphy pen with broad-edged nib or rubber stamps
- Charms
- Decorative papers
- Disposable brush
- Fabric adhesive
- Family photos
- Fine-point drawing and illustration pen
- Gesso
- Inkjet printer
- Metallic thread
- Old book text
- Polyester batting
- Ribbon
- Stamp pad or acrylic paint
- Transfer paper
- Unprimed canvas

Method

1. Using acrylic ink and a disposable brush, paint a thin wash of color onto the unprimed canvas.
2. When dry, paint a smooth, thin layer of gesso over the wash.
3. Add more acrylic ink or paint to desired areas to create attractive background.
4. Add words to gessoed canvas with rubber stamps, handwriting, or calligraphy
5. Scan family photos and print onto transfer paper.
6. Iron transfer paper onto fabric to transfer images to fabric.
7. Back photos with paper or fabric for frame-like appearance. Machine- or hand-stitch to canvas.
8. Hand- or machine-stitch ribbon and trim over and under photos.
9. Add small bits of old book text, fabric, buttons, charms, and stickers with fabric adhesive or stitching.
10. Select fabric for backing. Machine- or hand-stitch to front, leaving small opening.
11. Insert batting and stitch opening closed.
12. Stitch around the outside of the central collage to secure the batting and frame the collage.

Age:
Age makes us most fondly hug and
retain the good things of this life, when
we have the least prospect of enjoying
them. —*Atterbury.*

Leaving Home

Claudine Hellmuth
11" x 15½"

*where we love is home—home
that our feet may leave, but not
our hearts.*

Oliver Wendell Holmes

Renowned collage artist Claudine
Hellmuth is a master with paper
and paint, but she was wary of
working with a needle and thread.

　With minimal sewing skills and
a few pieces of fabric, Claudine has
created a whimsical and easy quilt
that lets her own style shine
though. Working without any pre-
conceived notions on how to go
about making a quilt, she discovered new ways to approach old
tasks that even experienced quilters
may find helpful.

　When she was ready to stitch,
Claudine realized that she was so
new to sewing that she didn't have
any straight pins in her house. So
she stapled each piece in place
onto the backing fabric. "This
worked great for me because I
didn't have to worry about the pins
sticking me while I was sewing. . . .
I had never sewn any sort of quilt
before, and I was excited to see
that it could be more liberating
than I'd imagined. I had a wonderful time doing it and now I can't
wait to make more!"

Materials

- Acrylic gel medium or fabric glue
- Acrylic paint
- Book text
- Cotton fabric
- Embroidery floss
- Found handkerchief
- Image photocopies
- Quilt batting
- Stapler
- Tissue paper

Method

1. Select images and make paper copies.
2. Copy book text onto paper.
3. On background fabric, cut and arrange pieces to create a simple composition.
4. Glue down paper images to background fabric, using gel medium or fabric glue.
5. Pin or staple fabric in place and stitch to backing with embroidery floss.
6. Use straight stitch to create additional line drawings.
7. Draw arms and legs onto tissue paper and pin or staple in place.
8. Stitch over tissue paper drawing and gently tear tissue away when finished.
9. Measure your finished top and cut a piece of batting 1" larger on all sides.
10. Cut your backing fabric 2" larger on all sides.
11. With right side of backing fabric down, lay your batting onto the backing and fold the edges up around the batting, gift-wrap style. Clip any bulky fabric when folding corners.
12. Pin or staple in place and iron flat.
13. Lay quilt top onto folded backing and batting, right side up, and pin in place.
14. Stitch front to back, around edge of quilt top, through all three layers.

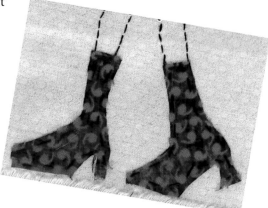

Mama with Chickens

12" x 14"

If I hadn't started painting, I would have raised chickens.

Grandma Moses

I was born and raised a city girl, just like my mama. However, when my mother was young, she spent summers on her grandpa's farm in Staunton, Virginia. This photograph was taken on that farm in 1931, when my mother was six years old.

When I was six, I was lucky enough to spend a weekend on that farm and get a little taste of the county and see where my mother grew up. I wanted to commemorate those memories for my mother, so I made this chicken quilt. I liked the little-girl feel of the pink chicken fabric. I added vintage farm images from my collection, which I printed onto fabric to set the mood and provide an environment for the photo. On the cow photo, I used photo-editing software to add some of my mama's farm-spun advice: "Why buy the cow if you can get the milk for free?" The same effect could be created by writing it with a fine-tipped permanent pen.

To demonstrate that a beautiful fabric quilt can be created without sewing a stitch, I assembled all of the fabrics, batting, and backing with fusible web.

Materials

- Acrylic matte medium
- Assorted fabrics
- Buttons
- Disposable brush
- Fabric adhesive
- Family photo
- Fine-point drawing and illustration pen
- Fusible batting
- Fusible interfacing
- Inkjet printer
- Inkjet transparency
- Pretreated fabric for inkjet printing
- Vintage farm images

Method

1. Select small pieces of fabric for quilt. Iron fusible interfacing to the back of each piece, following manufacturer's directions. Remove paper backing when cool.
2. Scan family photo and print onto inkjet transparency.
3. Transfer image to fabric (see Transferring Photos to Fabric, page 44).
4. Back photo with fusible interfacing. Remove paper backing when cool.
5. Scan and print vintage farm images onto pretreated fabric.
6. Back printed images with fusible interfacing and remove paper backing when cool.
7. Create a layered collage with fusible backed fabric.
8. Cut out farm images and complete the collage, framing the central photo. Pin in place.
9. Add text to image, using a fine-point drawing and illustration pen or photo-editing software.
10. When satisfied with arrangement, iron and fuse collage onto top layer, following manufacturer's directions.
11. Measure quilt top and cut fusible batting to size.
12. Iron fusible interfacing to fabric for quilt backing. Backing should measure 1½" larger than quilt top.
13. Remove paper from backing fabric when cool and stack quilt layers together.
14. Turn up backing to front around all sides of quilt, mitering corners. Iron down.
15. Iron quilt front and back to fuse layers together, following manufacturer's directions.
16. Stitch or glue on buttons, or little animal charms, to embellish.

Walk in the spirit

Mama always said, "Why buy the cow if you can get the milk for free?"

King Me

*The world is so full of a number
of things, I'm sure we should all
be as happy as kings.*

Robert Louis Stevenson

*I've always loved this photo of my
dad and his friends sitting on the
front steps of his grandmother's
house in the Washington, DC,
neighborhood of Mount Pleasant.
It's the very same house I was
brought home to when I was born.
Jack and his neighbors all look so
grown up in their Sunday best. I
thought they looked a little too
serious, so I added some party hats
to give the photo a whimsical
appeal. I chose the primary shapes
and colored fabrics to accentuate
this playful theme.*

*I transferred the image to
fabric, using the water-transfer
method, then machine-appliquéd
the hats. I used a topstitch thread
and needle to give the stitches
more dimension and to emphasize
their linear quality. The King's
crown-side of the checkers were the
perfect embellishment to reinforce
the message and add another
punch of primary color and shape.
They were glued on, then secured
with a big cross-stitch of hand-
dyed pearl cotton. The quilt was
bound by fusing squares of fabric
folded over the edge to create a
zigzagged edge of triangles.*

Materials

- Assorted decorative cotton prints
- Embroidery needle
- Family photo
- Fabric adhesive
- Fusible batting
- Fusible interfacing
- Glossy photo paper
- Hand-dyed pearl cotton
- Inkjet printer
- Muslin fabric
- Old checkers
- Red cotton duck
- Spray bottle (fine)
- Topstitch thread
- Water
- White polished-cotton fabric
- Workable fixative spray

Method

1. Scan photo and print onto photo paper.
2. Transfer photo to fabric, using the inkjet water method (see Water Transfers, page 48).
3. Let dry and spray with fixative to set inks.
4. Choose a fabric for the quilt top.
5. Select fabric to frame or back the photo—and a coordinating piece to back the checkers.
6. Cut triangular party hats from coordinated fabrics.
7. Print or stamp quote onto prepared muslin.
8. Cut batting to size of quilt top.
9. Cut backing to size of quilt top.
10. Stitch through all layers, using topstitch thread and needle.
11. Iron fusible interfacing to edging fabric; cut enough 1½" squares to go around quilt edge.
12. Fold squares on the diagonal and iron onto quilt edge, overlapping to cover edges.
13. Glue checkers to quilt with fabric glue.
14. When glue is dry, secure checkers with pearl cotton, using a big X stitch.

The world is so full of a number of things, I'm sure we should all be as happy as kings.
Robert Louis Stevenson

The Effects of Time

And so the hand of time will take The
fragments of our lives and make out
of life's remnants, as they fall, A
thing of beauty, after all.

Douglas Malloch

I love the patinas that come with
age: yellowed paper, rusted metal,
verdigris on copper, and cracked,
peeling paint. These signs of age
hint at untold stories.

Here, I've used painted
patinas and paper ephemera to
create a story for the unknown
woman in the photograph. The
rusted background and frame
were created by a two-step
antiquing solution.

The decorator remnant I
found was heavy enough to
serve as the combined border
and backing fabric. It echoes the
raised texture in the rusted wall-
paper frame, the curves in the
lace, and the script R appliqué.
The hard edges of all of the rec-
tangles are softened by those
curves which, with the addition
of the scalloped edging, provide
a visually exciting juxtaposition.

Materials

- Antiquing or rusting solution and rust antiquing solution
- Decorator remnant
- Embossed wallpaper
- Fabric adhesive
- Heavy-weight backing fabric
- Inkjet printer
- Instant coffee
- Jumbo rickrack
- Lace scrap
- Monogram appliqué
- Paper ephemera
- Pretreated fabric for inkjet printing
- Soft gel medium
- Unprimed canvas
- Vintage photo

Method

1. Cut a piece of unprimed canvas and wallpaper larger than the final finished size you need. Following manufacturer's directions, paint unprimed canvas and wallpaper with Metallic Iron paint, usually two coats, drying between coats.

2. Apply rusting solution to painted surfaces; cover the entire surface or just selected areas.

3. Cut rusted fabric to desired size for quilt top.

4. Adhere selected paper ephemera to rusted background fabric with soft gel medium.

5. Apply additional coat of gel medium to top of papers to increase durability.

6. Scan and print selected photo onto pretreated fabric.

7. Arrange photo and lace scraps over paper ephemera and stitch, fuse, or glue down.

8. Determine finished size of rusted frame. With a piece of scrap paper as a template, cut an opening that will encompass selective areas of your collage. When satisfied, cut rusted wallpaper and opening to size.

9. Machine-stitch or glue wallpaper frame to quilt top.

10. Mix a few grains of instant coffee with water to make a small puddle of coffee. With finger or brush, apply dabs of the coffee to tone down the whiteness of the photo and monogram initial—to give them the appearance of age.

11. Fuse, glue, or stitch monogram over corner of frame.

12. Using jumbo rickrack and fabric glue, glue one side of rickrack behind rusted fabric quilt top, making sure that the opposite edge presents as a scallop.

13. Cut backing fabric to a size that provides a nice border and frame for the finished quilt top.

14. Machine-stitch or glue quilt top to backing fabric.

Winter Morn

An early-morning walk is a blessing for the whole day.

Henry David Thoreau

Laura Cater-Woods is an award-winning quilter and teacher who likes to start her day with a walk along the river near her Montana home.

Digital photographs of the seasonal changes were printed onto four different fabrics: just before the light begins to come up, on silk dupioni (top left); a rosy dawn, on cotton poplin (bottom left); ripples on ice, on cotton broadcloth (top right); hoarfrost on twigs, on silk chiffon (bottom right). Photographs were pieced together with hand-dyed and batik fabrics to form the quilt top.

Transparent fabrics, fibers, and cocoon strippings were fused to the quilt top to suggest the movement and sparkle of light and water. The layers were further enhanced and integrated with free-motion embroidery using metallic and rayon threads. Color adjustments were made with watercolor pencils set with acrylic matte medium. The four photographs are so well integrated with the other fabrics and stitching that the quilt presents one large, seamlessly integrated landscape. Only upon closer inspection does one discern the individual photos.

Materials

- Acrylic matte medium
- Angelina® fibers
- Bonding powder or fusible
- Cocoon strippings
- Commercial batik fabric
- Digital or scanned photos
- Fusible interfacing
- Hand-dyed silk
- Inkjet printer
- Parchment paper
- Pretreated fabrics for inkjet printing
- Quilt batting
- Silk chiffon
- Watercolor pencils

Method

1. Select photos; print onto pretreated fabric.
2. Piece together photos with batik and hand-dyed silk to create quilt top.
3. Select area for transparent layering; cut silk chiffon large enough to cover area.
4. Place Angelina fibers, hand-dyed silk, and frayed cocoon strippings under chiffon as desired.
5. Sprinkle chiffon with bonding powder or fusible.
6. Cover powdered areas with parchment paper; iron to bond layers.
7. Cut batting and backing fabric to size of quilt top, plus 1" all around to allow for fabric uptake.
8. Using metallic and/or rayon threads, free-motion-machine-embroider the quilt top.
9. Square-up and trim quilt top, batting, and backing.
10. Bind edges with sewn or fused binding.

Open Heart – An Art Journal

Karen Michel
6½" x 9½"

> Art offers sanctuary to everyone willing to open their hearts as well as their eyes.
>
> Nikki Giovanni

Karen Michel reveals her true heart in everything she does. She is an accomplished mixed-media and altered-book artist and a dedicated teacher. Her distinctive use of rich, bright colors and simple iconic shapes infuses her art with an outward feeling of playfulness and an inner spirituality. Using rich red velvet, colorful silk scraps, and bold embroidery stitching, Karen created a small quilt that speaks volumes. She chose to affix it to an old book she rescued and rebound. It is now a book of blank pages waiting for someone to pour their heart into. You may choose to glue or machine-stitch this petite quilt—just remember to add your heart.

Materials

- Acrylic paint
- Aluminum tacks
- Assorted cotton, silk, and velvet scraps
- Awl
- Craft glue
- Embroidery floss
- Gel pens
- Gesso
- Hammer
- Hand-dyed silk ribbon
- Old book
- Several sheets of paper
- Small paintbrush
- Unprimed canvas

Method

1. Remove pages from old book and reinforce spine inside book by gluing additional paper to it for support.
2. Prime book with gesso.
3. Paint book cover with thin layers of acrylic paint, letting each layer show through in selected areas.
4. Create a small signature for the book by folding paper in half and cutting to fit inside book.
5. Using embroidery floss, stitch book signature through spine with basic bookbinding stitch.
6. Cut velvet to heart shape and stitch to a slightly larger piece of background fabric.
7. Cut flame shape from contrasting fabric.
8. Stitch flame to background with slightly contrasting embroidery floss to provide some variation in color.
9. Embroider eye onto heart in a freehand style, "drawing" the eye with colored threads.
10. Layer and stitch two or more fabrics behind heart collage using embroidery floss.
11. Cut unprimed canvas to fit behind; frame completed quilt.
12. Prime canvas with gesso and dry.
13. Paint canvas with acrylic paint to complement or contrast with quilt. Dry the canvas.
14. Stitch quilt to canvas with embroidery floss and needle.
15. Glue canvas to book cover.
16. Tack canvas to book cover with aluminum tacks to reinforce.
17. Hammer back side of tacks flat on inside of book cover.
18. Write word on book cover with gel pens.
19. Using awl, punch hole ¼" from side edge and halfway down front and back book covers.
20. Thread silk ribbon through holes and knot inside covers to provide decorative book closure.

Butterfly Girls

Olivia Thomas
15" x 12"

Happiness is like a butterfly which, when pursued, is always beyond our grasp, but, if you will sit down quietly, may alight upon you.

Nathaniel Hawthorne

Olivia Thomas is a fiber and mixed-media artist who creates under the name Olive Rose. She draws on her skills as a professional tailor to create well-executed works of art in a folk art style. Her recent efforts to work in a more organic and spontaneous style led Olivia to create this whimsical quilt that was inspired by some butterfly images in her collection. The photo of her mother as a young girl contrasts with the baby photo of Olivia. Appliquéing them both on the same brown fabric suggests that one never strays too far from a mother's sheltering wings.

New and vintage fabrics, as well as coffee-dyed linen, were used to create this folk art look. The polka-dot pattern of the border pieces is repeated in the smaller dot prints that ground the mother-and-daughter images —and which is echoed in the buttons and beads. The circle theme is further enhanced with the gold circles on the vertical scrap of fabric.

Materials

- Black tulle
- Buttons
- Embroidery floss
- Family photos
- New and vintage cottons
- Old packing string
- Pearl beads
- Quilt batting or flannel
- Vintage linen
- Vintage silk thread

Method

1. Select images and text and transfer to fabric (see Transfers, page 44), or print directly to fabric.
2. Lightly coffee-dye selected areas of linen to give it an aged look.
3. Create layered collage with assorted fabrics.
4. Cover fabric collage with tulle, and hand-stitch to linen over all layers.
5. Attach images and text over linen and tulle with tiny hand-stitches.
6. Stitch on beads and buttons.
7. Stitch additional fabrics to lower edge of linen.
8. Stitch on decorative string if desired.
9. Cut four strips of fabric approximately 1 ½" wide to create a border behind linen; pin in place. Hand- or machine-stitch around edge of linen to attach border.
10. Cut batting slightly smaller than quilt top.
11. Create quilt sandwich with top, batting, and backing (right side down), and stitch front-to-back around edge, encasing batting.

JUST A DREAM.

Ahhh, be still my beating wings.

1924/2004

My father didn't tell me how to live; he lived, and let me watch him do it.

Clarence B. Kelland

My dad serves as a daily reminder to me that life is what you make it, and that age is no reason to slow down or give up on your dreams.

This quilt was made simply, and it's an easy way to commemorate a special event in a loved one's life. The metal "Journey" tag at the bottom suggests the passing of time from 1924—when the childhood photo was taken—to 2004. The metal circle ties the two eras together—the circle of life. I printed two photos of my dad onto prepared fabric and framed them with green fabric to complement the outdoor setting of the photos.

I used pencils on the black-and-white photo to add more color. I chose black-and-white fabrics for the backgrounds so that the black-and-white photograph didn't stand out. The color scheme lends a strong, masculine tone to the piece. The use of the floral fabric behind the quote adds a punch of color to prevent the quilt from being too drab, and the green/gold brocade behind that colorful piece balances the colored metal embellishments.

Materials

- Assorted fabric scraps
- Embroidery needle
- Family photos
- Fusible interfacing
- Gold thread or embroidery floss
- "Journey" tag
- Larger pieces of fabric for quilt top and backing
- Pretreated fabric
- Quilt batting
- Round metal frame

Method

1. Scan and print family photos onto pretreated fabric and back with fusible interfacing.
2. Add color to enhance black-and-white photo and cut to size.
3. Choose fabric to frame photos and fuse photos to fabric.
4. Print quote or message onto pretreated fabric and back with fusible interfacing.
5. Cut out quote and choose one or two fabrics to frame quote. Fuse quote to fabric.
6. Stitch fabrics with fused photos and quote to larger fabric piece.
7. Attach brass circle frame, overlapping both photos, hand-stitching with gold thread or embroidery floss.
8. Attach brass "Journal" tag with supplied brads, or glue to fabric.
9. Select fabrics for quilt top and backing; cut to desired size along with a piece of batting.
10. With batting as bottom layer, and fabric arranged on top of batting with right sides together, pin all three layers together.
11. Sew quilt sandwich on all sides ¼" from edge, leaving a 4"–5" opening along the center of one side.
12. Trim away bulk of seams and batting, except at opening. Trim corners diagonally.
13. Turn quilt sandwich inside-out and iron to give sharp crease to edges.
14. Trim batting at opening and turn in fabric edges to align with sewn edge. Iron flat and hand-stitch closed.
15. Center and pin large fabric piece with collaged photos onto quilt "pillowcase."
16. Stitch around this piece ½" from edge of fabric.
17. Stitch around quilt "pillowcase" ½" from outer edge to create a frame and finished look.

Family faces are
magic mirrors.
Looking at people
who belong to us,
we see the past, present
and future. We make discoveries
about ourselves.
Gail Lumet Buckley

JOURNEY

Wings

when we make such a leap of faith, it is the actual stepping out that creates a bridge to see us safely to the other side.

Soren Kierkegaard

I am always inspired by this image. It reminds me of the possibilities that exist within us all; the potential we have to soar. I created this quilt as a study in color and construction. I wanted to make a little bed of quilt pillows—bound by ribbon—to frame this special image and experiment with my two current favorite colors, orange and purple. I wanted to create a relief-like effect because I had a unique display planned for this quilt—a vintage cutlery tray I rescued from an estate sale. The warm tones of the aged wood and worn green paint are echoed in the vintage ribbon and velvet millinery leaves.

Turquoise crystal beads add just the right amount of eye candy. Hand-stitching shows the hand of the maker, giving the quilt a personal touch and keeping the piece from being too sophisticated for its humble setting.

Materials

- Copyright-free image
- Four crystal beads
- Inkjet printer
- Pretreated fabric for inkjet printing
- Quilt batting
- Ribbon, 2"-wide
- Seven fabric scraps approximately 9" x 12" and smaller, in coordinating colors
- Six Velcro self-adhesive fasteners
- Velvet millinery leaves
- Vintage cutlery tray

Method

1. Scan and print image on pretreated fabric.
2. Pair image with backing fabric.
3. Pair remaining fabrics to create four pillowcase quilts; cut to successively larger sizes.
4. Cut a piece of batting to the size of each pillowcase quilt.
5. With batting as bottom layer, and fabric arranged with right sides together, pin all three layers together.
6. Sew each quilt sandwich on all sides ¼" from edge, leaving a 2"–3" opening along the center of one side of each.
7. Trim away bulk of seams and batting, except at opening, and trim corners diagonally.
8. Turn quilt sandwich inside-out and iron to give sharp crease to edges.
9. Trim batting at opening; turn in fabric edges to align with sewn edge. Iron flat and hand-stitch closed.
10. Add decorative hand-stitching to attach two bottom quilt pillows together.
11. Sew beads onto third quilt, also attaching that quilt to the ones below it.
12. Measure ribbon to go around the three bottom quilts. Cut and stitch together so that it slips onto quilt stack. Slip ribbon onto quilt stack and position.
13. Glue or stitch leaves to ribbon.
14. Stitch top quilt pillow (with image) to the layer beneath it.
15. Assemble Velcro fasteners, placing matching hook and loop sides together, with adhesive sides on outside.
16. Attach one adhesive side of Velcro fasteners to quilt back, three across top of quilt, three along the bottom.
17. Place quilt into well-cleaned and dry cutlery tray; use pressure to secure back of Velcro fasteners to tray. Leave in place 24 hours before attempting to remove quilt from tray to let adhesive set.

Love you, mean it

Fulvia Luciano
19" x 13½"

Mix a little foolishness with your serious plans: it's lovely to be silly at the right moment.

Horace

Fulvia Luciano is an accomplished photographer and fiber artist with the personal philosophy "Why shout when you can whisper." She prefers to say as much as she can, using as few elements as possible to achieve that goal. Here, the overall look of simplicity is actually comprised of a myriad of techniques that creates a complex background fabric. These surface design techniques are done in soft colors that don't compete with the focal point of the piece—the black-and-white photographs.

Fulvia's ideas start with a search through the collection of photographs she's taken to find a picture of people, a place, or event that she wants to memorialize. She likes to play around with size by enlarging, reducing, or inventively cropping the photos on her photocopier to help her determine the final composition. However, the real fun comes when she creates the background fabric. Working on unprimed canvas or muslin, Fulvia washes and steam-irons the fabric to get rid of any finishes that may interfere with the paints or dyes.

Using stamps, stencils and unusual mark-making tools like kitchen gadgets, Fulvia begins her surface design technique by randomly stamping shapes with acrylic paint on the dry fabric. Since the work will not be washed, she also uses crayons, watercolor pencils, markers, and dyes. The goal is to have fun and experiment.

For this quilt, Fulvia first laid out a makeshift grid by writing the words "TIC TOC TIC TOC" all over the background using a permanent ultrafine marker. The words intersect and cross all over the piece. Using acrylic paint and a small brush, she painted XOXOXO marks across the entire piece, and used the same paints to add additional random splotches of color.

Photos and text were printed on her inkjet printer on prepared fabric, and framed with a stronger color of felt to make them stand out from the background. After their placement was decided, she set them aside for further machine- and hand-stitching.

The quilt was then assembled with batting and backing. More Xs and Os were free-motion-stitched on the machine to secure the layers and add more texture. Then the photographs and background felt were machine-stitched into place. Once the original idea for the quilt was complete, Fulvia thought it needed even more texture. She used embroidery floss to hand-stitch a few more Xs and Os and splotches of color.

It's always better to place a few marks here and there and then reexamine the work from a distance of time and space to gain per-

spective. It's much easier to add embellishments than to remove them. Fulvia's decision to add more hand-stitched marks was just the right finish to this playful piece.

Materials

- Acrylic paints
- Assorted stamps, stencils, and mark-making tools
- Backing fabric
- Cotton muslin
- Embroidery floss
- Family photographs
- Felt
- Inkjet printer
- Permanent marker
- Pretreated fabric for inkjet printing
- Quilt batting

Method

1. Wash and press muslin. Cut muslin 2" larger than desired finished size.

2. Scan photos and quotes and print onto pretreated fabric.

3. Paint, stamp, write, and draw marks as desired onto background fabric.

4. Cut batting and backing to desired size of finished quilt.

5. Create quilt sandwich of printed top, batting, and backing.

6. Quilt layers together by adding additional marks with free-motion-machine- and hand-stitching.

7. Back photographs with felt to give a framed look.

8. Sew photographs and quotes to quilt backing.

9. Turn edges of quilt front around to back, and fold under to create a finished edge. Pin and iron in place and machine- or hand-stitch down.

Writer's Block

Patricia Bolton
9" x 12"

Put your ear down close to your soul and listen hard.

Anne Sexton

Artists usually create in isolation, and it can sometimes be a lonely and frustrating experience. However, art, especially quilting, has a way of bringing people together through the Internet, magazines, and gatherings of like-minded souls who instantly understand us. Patricia (Pokey) Bolton has created a quilt that mirrors both sides of being an artist. Writer's Block expresses her love of and frustration with writing, but also the glow that comes with pursuing what you love and gathering with others who share that passion.

As a base for her quilt, Pokey chose commercial decorator fabric that she had overdyed with fiber reactive dyes.

To break up the surface and add interest, she stamped the background with metallic paint. The transferred text was hand-stitched with a green metallic thread that picks up the green in the background and binding. Another green highlight was added with vintage velvet leaves. A ceramic butterfly embellishment adds an elegant finishing touch.

Materials

- Acrylic gel medium
- Embellishment
- Fabric scraps for transfers and stamping
- Felt for backing
- Fusible interfacing
- Inkjet printer
- Inkjet transparency
- Ink pad
- Metallic embroidery floss
- Pearlescent paint
- Photo and clipart
- Pretreated fabric for inkjet printing
- Rubber stamp
- Rotary cutter
- Vintage leaves

Method

1. Iron fusible interfacing to background fabric and cut to desired finished size.
2. Fuse background to felt backing.
3. Using pearlescent paint, stamp background fabric.
4. Print text onto transparency (remember to mirror-image print).
5. Transfer text to fabric with acrylic gel medium.
6. Scan and print photo and clipart onto pretreated fabric.
7. Back printed images with fusible interfacing; cut out.
8. To create border and soften edges, paint photo edges with pearlescent paint.
9. Back fabric scraps with fusible interfacing, then stamp image with permanent ink. Cut out.
10. Decide on placement of photos and text; layer additional fabric scraps for pleasing arrangement.
11. Fuse images to quilt.
12. With metallic embroidery thread and embroidery needle, stitch quotes to quilt with simple running stitch.
13. Back binding fabric with fusible interfacing. Cut four lengths ¾" wide and long enough to cover the edges of your quilt plus ½", using pinking shears.
14. Where the strips meet at the quilt corners, leave one about ½" beyond the edge and cut the other one at the quilt's edge.
15. Fold binding over quilt edges and fuse to quilt.
16. Fold corner edges of binding to back; fuse or glue.

Writer's Block

An idea that is not dangerous is unworthy of being called an idea at all.
Oscar Wilde

"The first step is to find out what you love -- and don't be practical about it. The second step is to start doing what you love immediately, in any small way possible. I've seen what happens to people when they get to do what they love. They light up. They glow. They have a kind of energy that's wonderful."
--Barbara Sher

If you wait for inspiration, you're not a writer, but a waiter.
Anonymous

Something Strange

14" x 18"

John Duns Scotus, born in Duns, Scotland, was a well-respected 13th-century scholar who thought that conical hats actually increased learning potential. The logic behind the cap was that it makes slow pupils learn better. However, Scotus later fell out of intellectual favor, and the Duns "dunce" cap was subsequently used to humiliate student wearers and motivate them to try harder.

I love the image on this quilt and use it often as a reminder to myself and others that there is nothing wrong with appearing strange. In a world where everyone is taught to conform, it's important to remember that all originality is a result of being different, and that it's an important ingredient for creativity.

I overpainted the black-and-white star fabric with fluid acrylics and a metallic acrylic craft paint to coordinate with the colors in the floral and green checkered fabric. The brown and cream brocade frames my vintage lace and photo focal point. The addition of the quote reinforces my intended message.

Materials

- Backing fabric
- Bead
- Button
- Four or five coordinating fabrics
- Hand-dyed rayon ribbon
- Heavy thread
- Inkjet printer
- Pretreated fabric for inkjet printing
- Quilt batting
- Staple gun
- Stretcher bars
- Vintage lace

Method

1. Scan and print photo and quote onto pretreated fabric.
2. Choose bottom layer of quilt top and allow about 5" extra all around to mount on stretcher bars.
3. Layer subsequent fabrics and lace on quilt top with photo as final layer.
4. Cut quilt backing and batting to same size as quilt top.
5. Lay quilt top on batting and backing.
6. Pin through all layers and hand- or machine-stitch around all the fabric edges, working from the center outward.
7. Stitch quote to quilt.
8. Fold a length of ribbon back-and-forth and tie in loose knot.
9. Machine- or hand-stitch ribbon to quilt.
10. Stitch button and bead on top of ribbon knot through all layers with heavy thread.
11. Assemble stretcher bars.
12. Position quilt evenly over stretcher bars; pull additional fabric around to back and place one staple in the center of each side.
13. Confirm placement of quilt on stretcher bars and adjust if necessary.
14. Staple quilt to stretcher bars, starting from center of each side.

Be true to your own act and congratulate yourself
if you have done something strange and extravagant
to break the monotony of a decorous age.
Ralph Waldo Emerson

Time & Again

Rayna Gillman
9" x 12"

*Time and memory are true
artists; they remold reality
nearer to the heart's desire.*

John Dewey

*To evoke a sense of past and
memory, of faded and layered
old walls and peeling bill-
boards, Rayna Gillman started
with her own hand-dyed fabrics.
She printed, screened, and
transferred images onto several
pieces, then pieced them
together to form an integral
whole. The result is a beautiful
melange of color and image
that recalls an earlier time.*

*The repetition of the arches
draws us into the quilt as if we
are stepping through the door-
way of time. This effect was
created by stamping a piece
of fabric with the paint left
on a plastic squeegee Rayna
had used to screen another
print. She simply turned it over
and stamped with it—typical
of the way she prints using
found objects.*

*The myriad layers and
techniques hold our interest as
we sift through both Rayna's
memories and our own past.
The combination of techniques
and hand-stitching creates
layers of depth that mimic the
layers of memory.*

Materials

- Acrylic matte or gel medium
- Cotton ball
- Hand-dyed fabric
- Inkjet copies
- Inkjet printer
- Inkjet transparency
- Quilt batting
- Solvent
- Spoon
- Squeegee or old credit card
- Stretcher bars or prestretched canvas
- Textile dyes, inks, and paint
- Thermal screen printing screens
- Toner copies of old newspaper

Method

1. Several methods were used to print or transfer the images:

   MAN – Thermal screen-printed with textile ink

   WATCH FACES – Thermal screen-printed with textile ink

   TEXT (bottom left) – Thermal screen-printed with thickened fiber-reactive dyes then washed in hot water to fade. A second layer was printed over that with a thermal screen made from Rayna's great-grandfather's passport, using textile ink.

   BILLBOARD (upper left) –

   a. Toner copies of old newspaper clippings were transferred with solvent applied with a cotton ball and burnished with a spoon (see Toner Transfers on page 50).

   b. Poster images were printed in reverse on Inkjet printer and coated with matte medium; placed face down on the fabric, burnished with a spoon and quickly removed, leaving part of the paper backing to give the look of peeling posters.

   c. Using solvent, apply another layer of newspaper clippings to the paper remaining from the poster image transfer.

   d. The old factory photo was printed onto an Inkjet transparency. A layer of soft gel medium was applied to the quilt and the transparency was burnished onto the fabric and on top of the peeling poster transfers.

2. Trim printed fabrics to size and piece together by hand or machine.

3. Trim quilt plus ¼" seam allowance on all sides to the size of the stretcher bars or canvas.

4. Sew 2" border strips of coordinating fabric to all sides.

5. Layer with batting and add hand-stitching.

6. Position quilt onto stretcher bars or canvas. Pull border strips around to back and staple to frame, starting from center of each side.

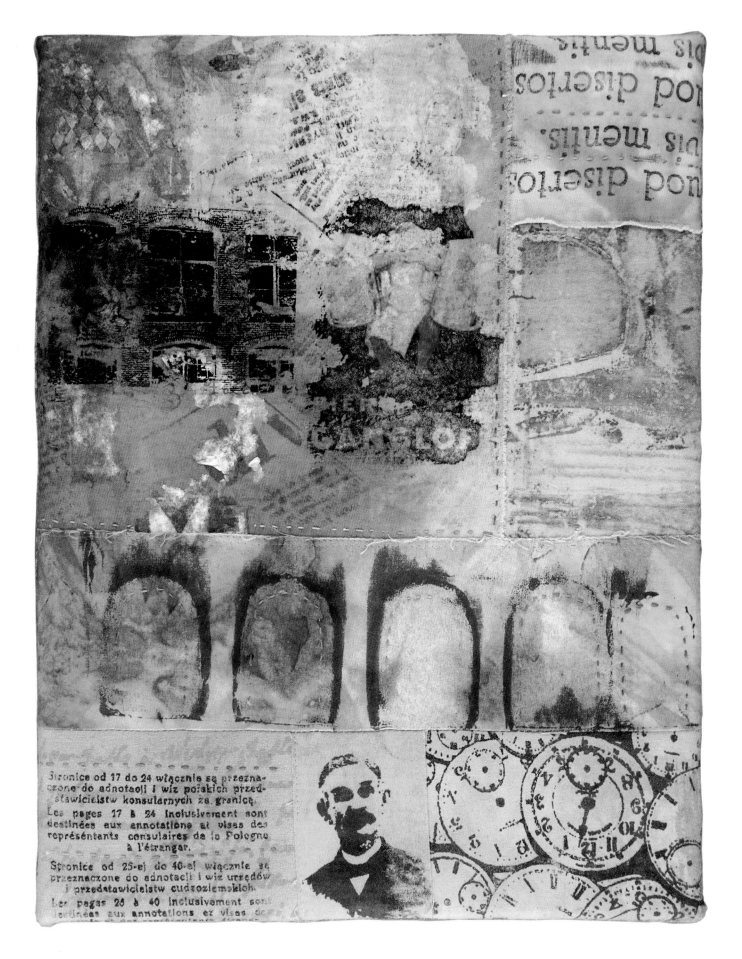

Fusion

The family is one of nature's masterpieces.

George Santayana

Janelle Girod began using photos in her work in 1999 when her interest in genealogy and preserving family photographs intertwined with her love of fibers and embellishments. Jan now creates quilts from fibers, fabrics, and fancy stitches that parallel what scrapbookers are doing with paper, stickers, and stamps.

Janelle found photos of her mom, dad, and herself taken when all three were about the same age. To convey a feeling of time and distance, she printed the images of her parents on both China silk and silk organza. She then used the sheer organza as an overlay on the China silk. Another method Janelle used to convey time was to cut out the photos and quotes, using a wood-burning tool to create a darkened irregular edge.

With layers of velvet and handmade paper as her base, Jan separated the quilt top into three sections with ribbon and rickrack. Three separate collages were created, one for each family member. They were embellished with family keepsakes that assist in the storytelling.

Materials

- Beads, buttons, charms
- Bubble Jet Set
- Cotton flannel batting
- Family photos
- Hand-dyed silks
- Heavy silk for binding
- Inkjet-pretreated silk
- Inkjet-pretreated silk organza
- Keepsake embellishments
- Metallic thread
- Paper
- Specialty threads, ribbons, rickrack
- Velvet
- Wood-burning tool

Method

Note: Prepare silk and silk organza for inkjet printing with Bubble Jet Set.

1. Scan, enhance, and resize photos.
2. Print quotes and photos on fabric.
3. Cut out photos and quotes, using wood-burning tool.
4. Fringe some hand-dyed silk to provide frames for the photos.
5. Create collage, using photos and ribbons; decide on placement of charms and mementos.
6. Layer rickrack over ribbon and stitch to quilt top to create three sections.
7. Layer organza over silk and attach both layers with decorative embroidery.
8. Complete all hand-embroidery and stitching of flat embellishments.
9. Layer quilt top with flannel batting and backing.
10. Machine-quilt around outer edges with metallic thread.
11. Complete embellishment by hand.
12. Square-up edges and bind quilt with heavier silk.

Moon... June... Spoon

Diane Herbort
11" x 14¾"

*The night walked down the sky
with the moon in her hand.*

Frederick L. Knowles

*Diane Herbort collects vintage
postcards, valentines, perfume
labels, and other ephemera. This
postcard was found in a shop in
Brussels a few years ago.
Combining it with the star-print
fabrics seemed natural right from
the start.*

*The addition of gold netting
in a curving swoop made her
think of shooting stars as well as
the moon. Gold-flecked organza
enhanced the moonlike feel.
Diane hand-stitched the netting,
and used a machine zigzag to
appliqué the organza in place.*

*A strong line of machine-
embroidered stars in gold metallic
thread, and two more lines of
smaller star designs in gold and
white, added just the right finishing touches, complementing the
overall theme.*

*With batting, but no backing
behind the top, Diane machine-
stitched curving lines of quilting
across the surface, first in blue,
then in gold metallic. The back was
pinned on the quilt and one more
line of quilting was added to hold
all three layers together.*

Materials

- Black-and-white toner photocopy of vintage postcard
- Cotton prints
- Fusible backing on release paper
- Gold pen
- Metallic and rayon threads
- Metallic netting
- Mother-of-pearl button and beads
- Organza
- Polyester batting

Method

1. Edge postcard with gold pen.
2. Select fabric that goes with the moon theme and create collage.
3. Hand- or machine-stitch postcard and fabrics to quilt top.
4. Add additional hand- or machine-embroidery.
5. Place batting under quilt top and add more stitching.
6. Stitch on star button and beads.
7. Add quilt backing and stitch an additional line to hold all layers together.
8. Bind.

School Days

The love of learning, the sequestered nooks, and all the sweet serenity of books.

Henry Wadsworth Longfellow

I collect grade-school ephemera and fabrics, anything that reminds me of a classroom. I challenged myself to create a collage quilt using as many photos as I could without it looking too busy. I needed a large focal point, so I made an inkjet transfer of one of my favorite photos. Because all of the photos are black-and-white, I kept the color scheme in the same black and white to help tie it all together.

The surrounding images are small enough that they don't draw attention away from the central figure, except for the class photo in the upper-right corner. To balance this large photo, I used the colorful line of pencils along the bottom, which adds weight to the overall design and just enough color and repetition to pull the eye back from the large photo. The fact that they all point upward sends the eye back up into the quilt and dancing around all of the images. The area of white space above the girl's head serves two functions: 1) provides a rest for the eye from all the movement and images; 2) emphasizes the idea that she is looking upward, searching for the answer.

Materials

- ABC twill tape
- Acrylic matte medium
- Bubble Jet Set
- Carpenter's wood glue
- Cotton canvas or duck
- Cotton fabric
- Cotton organdy
- Felt
- Fusible interfacing
- Inkjet printer
- Inkjet transparency
- Pretreated fabric for inkjet printing
- Vintage flash card
- Vintage photos
- Workbook page
- Worn pencils
- Zigzag rotary blade or pinking shears

Method

1. Scan and enlarge photo and flash card. Print onto inkjet transparency.
2. Scan and print photos on pretreated fabric or transparency.
3. Scan and print workbook page onto cotton organdy prepared with Bubble Jet Set.
4. On large piece of cotton canvas or duck, use transparency, photos and flash card to determine placement of collage elements.
5. With matte medium, transfer transparency photo to quilt top.
6. With felt serving as the middle and batting layer, layer quilt top, batting, and backing.
7. Stitch down background fabric, twill tape, workbook page, flash card, and photos.
8. Trim felt with zigzag edge.
9. Sew around edges of quilt top.

10. Working on a flat surface that you can leave undisturbed, use carpenter's wood glue to run a thin line of glue along one side of each pencil; and place them firmly onto quilt.
11. Leave quilt and pencils to dry flat overnight.

The Artist in Me

The object isn't to make art, it's to be in that wonderful state which makes art inevitable.

Robert Henri

It all began with the photograph, a vintage cabinet photo of an artist. It was a black-and-white photo that I colored with colored pencils (see Coloring black-and-white photos on page 56). I knew that now was the time to use my last piece of an old dishtowel I treasured for its beautiful bluebird border. I wanted the background fabric to blend with the landscape in the photo, so I took a sheet of script-printed tissue paper and fused it to fabric to make it more durable. I then painted over it with fluid acrylics and added highlights with white rubber-stamp ink. The sheer floral fabric allowed the script to show through, and it gave the outdoor feeling I was looking for. Metallic embroidered ribbon was the elegant accent for the quilt. Its pattern echoed the up-and-down movement of the birds in the dishtowel.

To make the photograph stand out, I sewed miniature piping around the edge and added an additional layer of batting under it before I stitched it onto the quilt top. The addition of some old paintbrushes I collect created a raised frame and emphasized the theme of the piece.

Materials

- Background and backing fabric
- Carpenter's wood glue
- Colored pencils
- Fluid acrylic
- Fusible interfacing
- Heavy thread
- Inkjet printer
- Large script tissue paper
- Metallic embroidered ribbon
- Miniature piping
- Old paintbrushes
- Ombré ribbon
- Pretreated fabric for Inkjet printing
- Quilt batting
- Sheer floral fabric
- Staple gun
- Stretched canvas
- Vintage photo
- Vintage textile remnants
- White cotton fabric
- White rubber-stamp ink pad
- Workable fixative spray

Method

1. Print vintage photo onto pretreated fabric.
2. Color in photo with colored pencils and spray with workable fixative to set colors.
3. Stitch piping to edge of photo.
4. Fuse interfacing onto white fabric.
5. Iron patterned tissue paper to smooth, and then fuse to white fabric.
6. Paint a wash of fluid acrylic onto tissue-paper fabric.
7. Crumble tissue-paper fabric to add wrinkles.
8. Smooth out and rub white rubber-stamp ink lightly over tissue paper's high points.
9. Create layered collage with remaining fabrics; pin in place.
10. Cut small piece of batting to size and place under photograph before pinning to quilt top.
11. Determine size of finished quilt. Cut a piece of coordinating decorative fabric, backing fabric, and batting large enough to create a border for collage; wrap around to back of stretched canvas.
12. From the bottom up, layer backing fabric, batting, background fabric, and fabric collage. Pin to hold layers.
13. Stitch fabric, ribbon, and collage layers, and around edge of tissue-paper fabric.
14. Adhere brushes to quilt, using carpenter's wood glue.
15. With needle and heavy thread, sew brushes onto canvas to add stability.
16. Center finished quilt on stretched canvas; bring edges around to back and staple in place.

True Meaning

The future belongs to those who believe in the beauty of their dreams.

Eleanor Roosevelt

Christine Adams is a button collector with a fondness for mother-of-pearl buttons. She is wise enough not to just let them accumulate in jars on her studio shelf. She knows how to put them to good use and make them shine like the little stars they are. In this button-quilted piece, she uses buttons to hold the quilt layers together as well as create a decorative frame for her central image and quote.

To create the green letters on yellow background, she used her word-processing software, setting the color of the page background to yellow and the text to green. She then printed on white inkjet-prepared fabric. The words were printed with enough spacing to enable her to cut them apart—ransom note style. The yellow background heightens the yellow in the vintage print, and the green lettering carries the planting theme, which is also reinforced by the green binding.

The random placement of the words and buttons prevents this simple composition from being too static and uninteresting.

Materials

- Backing fabric
- Buttons
- Copyright-free image
- Cotton fabric for quilt top and binding
- Fusible interfacing
- Inkjet printer
- Pretreated fabric for inkjet printing
- Quilt batting

Method

1. Scan and print photo and quote onto pretreated fabric.
2. Fuse interfacing to back of photo and quote.
3. Fuse photo to quilt top. Hand- or machine-stitch if desired.
4. Cut out words and fuse to quilt top. Hand- or machine-stitch if desired.
5. Layer quilt back, batting, and quilt top.
6. Stitching through all three layers, randomly sew on buttons.
7. Trim edges and bind quilt.

Spaghetti Sauce

Everything you see I owe to spaghetti.

Sophia Loren

I knew I wanted to make a quilt with this photo of my granddaughters in the kitchen getting ready to cook up some magic, but I was stuck for the longest time on what to do. I tried a vintage kitchen look, but the quilt just looked dull and predictable to me.

Weeks went by, and as my stash was tossed and turned while working on other quilts, up sprang a plaid silk that reminded me of the golden hues of sautéed onions and garlic. The red in the fabric whispered, spaghetti sauce— and there it was, the answer to my design dilemma.

Working with the plaid as the collage base, I pulled out the tomato-print fabric I had purchased years ago, thinking that I might need tomatoes someday. The selvage of a piece of gold fabric had numbers on it, reinforcing the idea of a recipe. The metal tomato buttons were waiting for me in my button collection. And the tomato vocabulary card? Serendipity!

Materials

- Assorted prints
- Backing fabric
- Family photo
- Novelty fabric and buttons
- Pretreated fabric for inkjet printing
- Quilt batting
- Vintage card
- Vintage trim

Method

1. Select fabrics for collage.
2. Scan family photo and print on pretreated fabric.
3. Create a layered collage with fabrics.
4. Measure quilt top and cut a piece of coordinating fabric for a pillowcase quilt 1½" inches larger on all sides to provide a border and frame for the collage.
5. Cut batting and backing fabric to same size as border.
6. Layer backing and top, right sides together, with the batting on top of these two fabrics. Stitch around the edges, leaving an opening to turn it inside out. Turn through opening and iron edges flat.
7. Hand-stitch the opening closed.
8. Lay collage on the top.
9. Cut four pieces of trim slightly longer than each side of collage.
10. Pin, fuse, or glue trim to edge of collage to hold in place.
11. Stitch down all fabrics, card, and trim through all layers of quilt.
12. Quilt around book, chef's hats, and girl's shirts to add dimension.
13. Stitch on buttons.

May Queen

For I'm to be Queen o' the May,
mother, I'm to be Queen o' the May.

Alfred Lord Tennyson

I was inspired by the 1941 photograph of my mother-in-law, Anne
McCeney Riley, as May Queen and
a fragile photo of her mother as
the May Queen.

I never knew the original
purpose of blue-and-white vintage
textile I purchased years ago.
Because of the colors, it was the
perfect background for my May
Queen collage. I used another blue-
and-white napkin from an estate
sale, a delicate scrap of dotted
swiss, some overdyed bark cloth,
and a length of vintage blue velvet
ribbon. I wanted to provide a frame
for the beautiful scalloped edge of
the vintage textile, so I sewed the
collage on a pillowcase quilt of
blue plaid.

The photographs are inkjet
water transfers. I manipulated the
colors in the small photo of Anne's
mother and printed several variations. It was fitting that they
appeared as a foundation, holding
up Anne's photo. The arrangement
holds even more significance when
you know that Anne's mother had
died the month before Anne was
crowned May Queen.

Materials

- Fabrics for collage
  backing and quilt
  backing
- Family photo
- Fiber-reactive dye
- Fusible interfacing
- Glossy photo paper
- Inkjet printer
- Quilt batting
- Spray bottle (mist)
- Vintage ribbon
- Vintage textiles
- Water
- Workable fixative spray

Method

1. Scan photos and print onto glossy photo paper.
2. Transfer photos to fabric, using the inkjet water method (see Water Transfers on page 48).
3. Let dry, then spray with fixative to set inks.
4. Overdye bark cloth with fiber-reactive dye.
5. Create collage with vintage textiles and photos.
6. Create a layered collage with fabrics.
7. Measure quilt top and cut a piece of coordinating fabric for a pillowcase quilt 1½" inches larger on all sides to provide a border and frame for the collage.
8. Cut batting and backing fabric to same size as border.
9. Layer backing and top, right sides together, with the batting on top of these two fabrics. Stitch around the edges, leaving an opening to turn it inside out. Turn through opening and iron edges flat.
10. Hand-stitch the opening closed.
11. Lay collage on the top and stitch down all fabrics and photos through all layers.

Doll Dresses

◎◎

we don't stop playing because we grow old; we grow old because we stop playing.

George Bernard Shaw

Did you save your old doll clothes for your daughter to play with? That's OK, neither did I. I don't remember playing with dolls; but then again, there I am in black-and-white holding one. I was reminded of that photo when I came across the one of my daughter in almost the same pose, holding her favorite doll. I rummaged through my collection of estate sale goodies to find the doll clothes that I was inspired to buy long before I ever conceived this quilt. You have to be prepared for any and all inspirations, right?

Black and white and red all over. The red doll dresses directed my color scheme. I converted the color photo of my daughter to black-and-white to carry through the color scheme, and I decided on a horizontal format to suggest the flow of time between the two photographs. When I saw how wide the quilt would be, I instantly thought that it would look good hanging over my daughter's bed, so I added narrow strips at the top to tie over a drapery pole.

Materials

- Assorted prints in brocade, cotton, rayon, and silk
- Drapery pole and finials
- Family photos
- Felt
- Pretreated fabric for inkjet printing
- Quilt batting
- Vintage doll dresses

Method

1. Select fabrics for collage.
2. Scan family photos and print on pretreated fabric.
3. Create a layered collage with fabrics, photos, and doll dresses.
4. Measure quilt top and cut a piece of coordinating fabric for a pillowcase quilt 2" larger on all sides to provide a border and frame for the collage.
5. Cut batting and backing fabric to same size as border.
6. Layer backing and top, right sides together, with the batting on top of these two fabrics.
7. Cut five strips approximately 3½" x 11" (or adjust to the quilt size).
8. Fold in half lengthwise and stitch ¼" from edge along the side and across bottom, leaving an opening for turning.
9. Turn inside out and press flat. Sew open edge closed.
10. Fold each strip in half. Starting about 1" from each edge and spacing evenly across the pillowcase quilt, pin folded edge of strip between right sides of backing and top fabrics with the long edges toward the center of this sandwich. Keep the folded edge of the strip flush with the outer edges of the backing and top fabric.
11. Stitch around edges, leaving an opening to turn right side out.
12. Turn right side out; hand-stitch the opening closed and press.
13. Set aside the doll dresses and pin photo collages and dress background fabrics on the top; stitch through all layers.
14. Arrange doll dresses and hand-stitch to quilt.

A Gallery of
Quilted Memories

**MORE IDEAS AND
INSPIRATION FROM
ARTISTS AND QUILTERS**

To give oneself as one is, to let life meet us as it really is, to live for the moment and extract from each moment all that it holds of truth, beauty and goodness, without scruple, without vain questioning, in the spontaneous desire of life, in childlike purity of heart ... to be able to be oneself, to dare to be happy and at last allow one's soul to spread its wings.

Jeanne de Vietinghof

WAITING (WITH WINGS)
Lesley Riley
13" x 23"

ROSES CAME TODAY
Jeanie Smith
8½" x 11"

A single rose can be my garden . . .
a single friend, my world.

Leo Buscaglia

it takes courage to grow up
and turn out to be who you really are.
ee cummings

COURAGE
Lesley Riley
10" x 12"

courage is contagious. When a brave man takes a stand, the spines of others are often stiffened.

Billy Graham

THE FLOWER GIRL
Lesley Riley
8" x 10"

Flowers have spoken to me more than I can tell in written words. They are the hieroglyphics of angels, loved by all men for the beauty of the character, though few can decipher even fragments of their meaning.

Lydia M. Child

FOURTH GENERATION QUILTS THE FIRST
Alan Kelchner
17" x 18½"

we need to remember across generations that there is as much to learn as there is to teach.

Gloria Steinem

ST. QUILTA BLESSES THE STUDIO
Susan (Lucky) Shie
10½" x 16½"

How blessings brighten as they take their flight.

Edward Young

PORTRAIT
Joanne Gerwig
10" x 12"

What a joy it is to capture the likeness of another human being. It has been said that the eyes are the window through which we glimpse the soul. That's my favorite thing to paint—souls!

Ann Manry Kenyon

TENDER HEART
Claudine Hellmuth
10" x 13"

For his heart was in his work, and the
heart giveth grace unto every art.

Henry Wadsworth Longfellow

INVOLVE ME
Christine Adams
13" x 16"

Grown-ups never understand anything by themselves, and it is tiresome for children to be always and forever explaining things to them.

Antoine de Saint-Exupery

*It is never too late to
be what you might
have been.*

George Eliot

LATE BLOOMER
Lesley Riley
15" x 22"

EVIDENCE OF FAMILY
Lesley Riley
10" x 15"

*Other things may change us, but
we start and end with family.*

Anthony Brandt

A ROOM OF HER OWN
Lesley Riley
12½" x 12"

*A woman must have money and a room
of her own if she is to write fiction.*

Virginia Woolf

FROM THE NEIGHBORHOOD
Lesley Riley
9" x 12"

we are made wise not by the recollection of our
past, but by the responsibility for our future.

George Bernard Shaw

SWEET
Lesley Riley
12" x 12"

Be sweet, be good, and honest always.

Emma Bunton

BALLERINA
Lesley Riley
12¾" x 17¼"

I wanted so badly to study ballet, but it was really all about wearing the tutu.

Elle Macpherson

Resources

Materials

AMERICAN TAG
www.AmericanTag.net
Commerce, CA 90040
800.223.3956
Home-Pro tool, rivets, eyelets

ART CLOTH STUDIOS
www.artclothstudios.com
1134 West Agarita
San Antonio, TX 78201
Thermofax screen preparation service

ARTFABRIK
www.Artfabrik.com
324 Vincent Place
Elgin, IL 60123
847.931.7684
hand-dyed fabric and threads

BO-NASH
www.bonash.com
800.527.8811
bonding powder

COLORTEXTILES
www.colortextiles.com
612.382.0013
inkjet printer fabric

DHARMA TRADING CO.
www.dharmatrading.com
654 Irwin St.
San Rafael, CA 94901
800-542-5227
textile craft supplies, dyes, fabric

EPSON AMERICA, INC.
www.epson.com
800.463.7766
printers, scanners, iron-on
transfer paper, photo paper, archival
& waterproof inkjet inks, transparencies for inkjet printers

FAIRFIELD PROCESSING
www.poly-fil.com
800.980.8000
batting

GOLDEN ARTIST COLORS, INC.
www.goldenpaints.com
607.847.6154
paints, fluid acrylic, acrylic mediums

HEWLETT-PACKARD
www.hp.com
800.752.0900
printers, scanners, digital cameras, transparencies for inkjet printers, photo paper, quilting and technology support

JET PRINT PHOTO
www.JetPrintPhoto.com
800.632.6023
multiproject glossy photo paper, graphic image paper matte finish

C. JENKINS COMPANY
www.cjenkinscompany.com
St. Louis, MO
Bubble Jet Set, inkjet printer fabric

JUNE TAILOR
www.JuneTailor.com
800.844.5400
fusible batting, inkjet printer fabric

KRYLON
www.krylon.com
fixatives, faux finishes, paints

PELLON
www.shoppellon.com
fusible interfacing

SANFORD
www.sanfordcorp.com
2711 Washington Blvd.
Bellwood, IL 60104
pencils, markers

SOPHISTICATED FINISHES BY TRIANGLE COATINGS
www.modernoptions.com
510.614.3900
antiquing and patina solutions

USARTQUEST
www.usartquest.com
7800 Ann Arbor Road
Grass Lake, MI 49240
mica

THE WARM COMPANY
www.warmcompany.com
206.320.9276
Warm and Natural batting

Designers

Christine L. Adams
Rockville, MD

Patricia Bolton
Stow, MA

Laura Cater-Woods
Billings, MT

Lisa Engelbrecht
Long Beach, CA

Joanne Gerwig
Freeland, MD

Rayna Gillman
West Orange, NJ

Janelle L. Girod
Marietta, GA

Gloria Hansen
Hightstown, NJ

Claudine Hellmuth
Orlando, FL

Diane Herbort
Arlington, VA

Alan R. Kelchner
San Francisco, CA

Fulvia Luciano
Brockton, MA

Karen Michel
Island Park, NY

Lynne Perella
Ancram, NY

Susan Shie
Wooster, OH

Jeanie Smith
Anchorage, AK

Olivia Thomas
Phoenix, AZ

Sources for additional information on techniques

Books

There are a number of books on computer/quilt techniques available by the following authors: Ann Johnston, Jean Ray Laury, Jane Dunnewold, Ruth Issett, Claudine Hellmuth, Lynne Perella and Gloria Hansen.

Magazines

Quilting Arts (www.quiltingartsllc.com)

Cloth Paper Scissors (www.quiltingartsllc.com)

Somerset Studio (www.stampington.com)

Legacy (www.stampington.com)

Fiberarts (www.fiberartsmagazine.com)

Surface Design Journal (www.surfacedesign.org)

Web sites

US Copyright Office
www.copyright.gov/

Inkjet Transfer Discussion Group
groups.yahoo.com/group/inkjet_transfers/

LaLas Land
www.LaLasLand.com
My Links Page lists Web sites of contributing artists and many other sources of interest to readers.

Gloria Hansen
www.gloriahansen.com

Metric Equivalency Charts

inches to millimeters and centimeters						
inches	mm	cm	inches	cm	inches	cm
⅛	3	0.3	9	22.9	30	76.2
¼	6	0.6	10	25.4	31	78.7
½	13	1.3	12	30.5	33	83.8
⅝	16	1.6	13	33.0	34	86.4
¾	19	1.9	14	35.6	35	88.9
⅞	22	2.2	15	38.1	36	91.4
1	25	2.5	16	40.6	37	94.0
1¼	32	3.2	17	43.2	38	96.5
1½	38	3.8	18	45.7	39	99.1
1¾	44	4.4	19	48.3	40	101.6
2	51	5.1	20	50.8	41	104.1
2½	64	6.4	21	53.3	42	106.7
3	76	7.6	22	55.9	43	109.2
3½	89	8.9	23	58.4	44	111.8
4	102	10.2	24	61.0	45	114.3
4½	114	11.4	25	63.5	46	116.8
5	127	12.7	26	66.0	47	119.4
6	152	15.2	27	68.6	48	121.9
7	178	17.8	28	71.1	49	124.5
8	203	20.3	29	73.7	50	127.0

yards to meters									
yards	meters	yards	meters	yards	meters	yards	meters	yards	meters
⅛	0.11	2⅛	1.94	4⅛	3.77	6⅛	5.60	8⅛	7.43
⅛	0.11	2⅛	1.94	4⅛	3.77	6⅛	5.60	8⅛	7.43
¼	0.23	2¼	2.06	4¼	3.89	6¼	5.72	8¼	7.54
⅜	0.34	2⅜	2.17	4⅜	4.00	6⅜	5.83	8⅜	7.66
⅝	0.46	2½	2.29	4½	4.11	6½	5.94	8½	7.77
⅝	0.57	2⅝	2.40	4⅝	4.23	6⅝	6.06	8⅝	7.89
¾	0.69	2¾	2.51	4¾	4.34	6¾	6.17	8¾	8.00
⅞	0.80	2⅞	2.63	4⅞	4.46	6⅞	6.29	8⅞	8.12
1	0.91	3	2.74	5	4.57	7	6.40	9	8.23
1¼	1.03	3¼	2.86	5⅛	4.69	7¼	6.52	9⅛	8.34
1¼	1.14	3¼	2.97	5¼	4.80	7¼	6.63	9¼	8.46
1⅜	1.26	3⅜	3.09	5⅜	4.91	7⅜	6.74	9⅜	8.57
1½	1.37	3½	3.20	5½	5.03	7½	6.86	9½	8.69
1⅝	1.49	3⅝	3.31	5⅝	5.14	7⅝	6.97	9⅝	8.80
1¾	1.60	3¾	3.43	5¾	5.26	7¾	7.09	9¾	8.92
1⅞	1.71	3⅞	3.54	5⅞	5.37	7⅞	7.20	9⅞	9.03
2	1.83	4	3.66	6	5.49	8	7.32	10	9.14

Index